A HELL OF A LIFE

FROM MANGER TO MEGASTAR

by John Dickson

FOR JOSH

Other publications by John Dickson:
Hanging in There
A Sneaking Suspicion
Zed Magazine

John can be contacted in cyber-space at:
zeded@ozemail.com.au

PO Box 225, Kingsford NSW 2032
Telephone (02) 9663 1478 Facsimile (02) 9662 4289
E-mail matmedia@ozemail.com.au

All illustrations by David Cornish
All photography by David Stowe
Typesetting and design by Joy Lankshear
Matthias Media
Printed in Australia

Many thanks...
Ian Powell, for not writing this book first.
My lecturers at Moore College, for teaching me how much I don't know.
Anne Mackenzie, for finding so many mistakes!
Philip Andrew, for the improvements.
Glenda Weldon, for first telling me the story.
Buff, for love at first sight.
Yeshua, for breath
Mum, for *everything!*

Contents

STRANGE BEGINNINGS

1 Jesus in Cyber-Space .... PAGE 9

2 Jesus Christ Superscam .... PAGE 15

3 Stranger than Fiction .... PAGE 21

4 The Strangest Fan Club in the World .... PAGE 27

THE GLORY DAYS

5 Jesus and Arnie .... PAGE 35

6 In the Event of an Emergency .... PAGE 41

7 Meeting the Megastar .... PAGE 49

8 What would Jesus say to Madonna? .... PAGE 57

9 To be Terminated .... PAGE 65

A HELL OF A WAY TO GO

10 God in our Shoes .... PAGE 73

11 Jesus' 'fatal flaw' .... PAGE 79

12 The Trial of your Life .... PAGE 85

13 A Hell of a Life .... PAGE 93

A SERIOUS COMEBACK

14 For those who like a Good Argument .... PAGE 105

15 Alive and Kicking .... PAGE 115

16 A Word from Jesus' Fans .... PAGE 123

Appendix: Where to find Jesus' words .... PAGE 128

STRANGE BEGINNINGS

"How on earth this baby boy ended up starring in movies, web pages and history's #1 best-seller, is beyond me – literally!"

JESUS IN CYBER-SPACE

IT **SEEMS** **TO** **ME** that whenever people have invented new technologies for communicating with each other, Jesus has been the first thing on our minds.

For example, when printing was invented five hundred years ago, the first book off the press was the one Jesus stars in—the Bible. In fact, many of the first few hundred different titles were ones that related to Jesus' life.

Movies are another example. Since 'moving pictures' were first invented, about a hundred years ago, there have been over 20 different movies made about Jesus' life. That's more than even James Bond has had.

But what about now? Has Jesus kept his popularity in the "cyber-90s"?

I decided to conduct an experiment to find out. I logged on to the Internet recently to search for information relating to Jesus. First though, I searched for 'web pages' relating to Michael Jordan and Madonna. I thought it would be interesting to compare Jesus' popularity in cyber-space with two of the most popular people on the planet today. Here are the results:

- Mike Jordan clocked up a huge 921 sites.
- To my surprise, Madonna dwarfed Mike (so to speak) with 2121 sites.
- Then I typed in 'Jesus Christ'. He outdid them both with 4515 sites— that's more than both of them put together.

I kept running searches through the different search engines, just to make sure of the results. Every time I did it, Jesus more than doubled the 'hits' of Mike and Madonna. Not bad for a man born in an animal shed almost 2000 years ago.

Some of my more cynical mates might say that this simply proves there are more 'computer nerds' out there who are Christians than there are computer nerds who are Mike and Madonna fans. That might be true of course, but I think it still shows what I said before—whenever we come up with a new way to talk about life, Jesus is one of the biggest topics on our lips—and our web pages.

But how on earth did Jesus get to be so popular? How did he go from being a carpenter in his dad's business, to having over 1,000,000,000 fans who think he's in charge of the universe? How did he advance from the manger to such mega-stardom? That question is sort of what this book is about.

If you'd asked me when I was a teenager, "How come Jesus is so popular?", I wouldn't have had a clue. My first impressions of this carpenter-turned-megastar came from Hollywood movies—the ones they repeat every Easter on TV. I must admit, I was never very impressed. For starters, he wore what looked like a dress or 'nighty', which for a teenage bloke was pretty hard to cope with. I'd just reached puberty—deeper voice, girls on the mind, hair in new places—so someone who wore long white robes in public was not my idea of a man's man! What's more, he

never seemed to smile. I'm not saying he looked depressed, it's just that he seemed to be in a constant daze. I couldn't help thinking he must have been very boring to be around. For a Year 9 guy these were critical issues. At this age, I was *tough* and *into fun.* Jesus, on the other hand, seemed *weak* and *boring.* That settled it: Jesus was not for me.

The silly thing was, I had never read any of the biographies about Jesus in the Bible—I didn't even know there were any. It never crossed my mind that the Hollywood movies might have got him wrong. It was pretty sad really, a billion people in the world today worship this man, and I'd almost made up my mind about him from a couple of tacky 1970s films.

Things changed though. At the end of Year 9 I got a new 'Scripture' teacher. I had never been able to work out these religious people. They came to my school once a week to talk about God and weren't even paid for it. Why on earth would someone do that? Especially since 'Scripture' was even less popular than 4 Unit Maths.

This new Scripture teacher did an amazing thing one day. She invited the class to come to her home on Friday afternoons for Bible study, hamburgers, milkshakes and scones. We were 15 year old blokes, so this was not a hard decision to make. We may not have been keen on the 'Bible', but we were definitely keen on the food. So, one Friday afternoon we turned up to her place and made ourselves at home. Sure enough, she made as much food as six teenagers can eat. Then, when we were too full to make a move, she brought out the Bible.

To my surprise, she never threw a rule book at us or said, "Cut your hair, tuck your shirt in, go to bed by nine, and be good Christian boys". Instead, she talked about Jesus, but in a way that sounded nothing like the man I'd seen in the movies or on Christmas cards. This was the Jesus straight out of the Bible, and he was amazing. He was funnier than I ever expected, tougher than I ever imagined, and stranger than anyone I'd come across. Within a couple of months of these Friday afternoon Bible studies I slowly became convinced that Jesus was at least as important as the hamburgers, milkshakes and scones, which for a 15 year old bloke was quite a step. Everything I had previously thought about him seemed ridiculous. Everything I began to learn about him captured my mind. "His was quite a life", I thought to myself, "a hell of a life".

If you had told me when I was a teenager that I would one day write a book about Jesus, I would not have believed you. But Jesus is like that —he has always had a way of attracting the most unlikely people. When he walked the dusty roads of ancient Palestine, it was not the "religious" people who flocked to him, but the "not-so-religious". It's my belief in this simple fact, that led to the writing of this book.

If you're already among the billion or so people who think Jesus runs the world, this book isn't really for you. It's great to have you along, but I must admit, this book is written more for people who can't quite see why there's so much fuss about him.

- It's for those who occasionally use his name—"ahh Jesus!"—but don't know how it came to be a swear word.
- It's for those who have seen a Jesus movie but, like me, thought he was a bit of a 'sandal-and-nighty-wearing-fairy…tale' from the past.

- It's for those who reckon Jesus was probably a 'good bloke' but wouldn't really count him among their mates.
- It's for those who list Jesus as one of the 'great teachers' but aren't real sure what he taught.
- It's for those who think Jesus was a lunatic, or a liar. It's even for those who doubt he ever existed.

If that sounds vaguely like you, thanks for reading. I hope you enjoy it.

CHAPTER

2

JESUS CHRIST SUPERSCAM

IN THE LAST FEW YEARS some very influential people (musicians, film directors and writers) have brought us 'fresh' looks at the life of Jesus. Andrew Lloyd Webber's musical, *Jesus Christ Superstar*, gave us an angry, misunderstood Jesus. Director Martin Scorsese's film, *The Last Temptation of Christ,* gave us the self-deluded, sexually-repressed Jesus. And more recently, academic Barbara Thiering's best selling book, *Jesus the Man,* gave us the married-with-three-kids-then-divorced Jesus.

THE OLD IMPROVED VERSION

Each of these presentations had one thing in common. Their picture of Jesus was based on anything but the traditional sources of our information about the man. In trying to be exciting and controversial they managed to create a version of Jesus that looks almost nothing like the one described in the original biographies of his life. This is sad really, especially since the Jesus presented in the four biographies (often called the 'Gospels' of Matthew, Mark, Luke, and John, named after the four men who wrote them) is far more exciting and controversial than any of the modern versions. In fact, the Jesus of the Bible (where these biographies are now preserved) makes the new versions of the man look like a collection of Ned Flanders' friends.

I must tell you up front, I have no intention of presenting a 'new', 'revised' Jesus. Instead, I'm going to stick with the thoroughly old one. In each chapter I'll give you a taste of what these ancient biographies say about the man. That way, whether you like what you see or not, at least you can make an informed decision about him. That's more than I was able to do as a teenager.

But this leads to a crucial question—can you trust these ancient biographies? After all, aren't they part of the Bible? With a little help from a chapter in my last book*, let me try to answer this question.

IS IT FICTION?

Actress Winona Ryder once said: "Religion is fiction. I've read the Bible. It's a great book, but it's a novel". I'm sure her opinion is shared by many others. In fact, probably the most common view of the Bible is just that— it's a book you respect but don't trust.

If you'd asked me at 15 what I thought of the Bible I would have answered something like, "It's irrelevant. It's historically unreliable. And on top of that, it's been changed through the years so you don't know what it originally said anyhow". Amazing isn't it? I had never actually read the Bible, wouldn't have had a clue how to test for historical

---

*My last book was called *A Sneaking Suspicion*. It's about the hunch we have that there's more to life than beer and footy.

reliability, and couldn't have told you what languages it had been trans-
lated from, but I would still have given such a confident reply!

Occasionally, people warn us not to believe the 'myths' about Jesus in
the Bible. The funny thing is, the real myths are the ones *about* the Bible not
in it. I want to look at a few of these myths which have become so common.

MYTH 1: IT'S BEEN 'LOST' IN THE TRANSLATION

How many times have you heard this argument:

> *The Bible was translated from one language to another, then into another and
> so on and on. By the time it got to our English, its original meaning was lost.*

The fact of the matter is that most Bibles available today are taken
directly from the original languages—Hebrew, Aramaic and ancient
Greek. Our knowledge of these languages is getting more and more
precise, which means that translations are actually getting more accurate,
not less. When I quote a section out of one of Jesus' biographies in this
book, you can be sure that what you're reading is a direct translation of
the Greek it was first written in.

The argument about 'losing it' in the translation process really is a myth.

MYTH 2: IT'S BEEN CHANGED

Then of course, some people argue that the scribes (those who copied
and passed on the ancient Bible documents) decided to make dramatic
changes to the stories to suit themselves. An example of this argument
might say that the famous walking-on-water story in Mark's biography
started out as Jesus 'swimming' in water. Then (according to this argument) some ancient scribe thought to himself, "That's a bit boring. I
know, I'll make it say Jesus walked on the water instead".

The problem with this view is the evidence—there isn't any. We have
in our possession hundreds of ancient copies of Mark's biography, found
in many different places all over the ancient world. Let's suppose for a
minute one bored scribe from Athens did decide to change Jesus' *swimming* into *walking* on water. Surely, you would still expect to find the

original swimming story in one of the many other copies we've uncovered. It's not as if the Athenian scribe could fax his changes through to his friends in Jerusalem or Rome and get them to make the changes too. The fact is, of all the ancient copies of Mark, only one version of this story exists and it says Jesus *walked* on water.

This is just one example, but the same principle can be applied to any of the amazing stories about Jesus' life. Without any evidence of what a scribe is supposed to have deliberately changed, it makes no sense to argue that he did so. Such a speculation is based on bias rather than evidence.

MYTH 3: IT CONTAINS ACCIDENTAL MISTAKES

Others argue:

OK! So maybe the scribes didn't make deliberate changes, but what about mistakes? What if, over the years, errors were accidentally over-looked? Surely that would make the Bible unreliable today.

The fact is 'mistakes' were made in some of the ancient copies of Jesus' biographies. Actually, I'll show you one.

The Gospel of Mark, chapter 5, begins with:

They (Jesus and his disciples) went across the lake to the region of the Gerasenes.

So what? The problem is, the various ancient copies (remember we've found heaps) differ on the spelling (in Ancient Greek, of course) of this region. Some have it "Gadarenes", others "Gergesenes", and still others the spelling I first quoted. Obviously, some scribe, somewhere, messed up. As a result, scholars now have to search through the many ancient copies of Mark and find out which is the most popular and reliable spelling. When they do, that's the one that appears in our English Bibles.

Of course, this isn't the only 'mistake' in these ancient biographies. In fact, there are many more, and some of them are more significant than this one. The important thing to know, however, is that in none of the 'mistakes' is the meaning of Jesus' life changed, lost, or distorted.

TELLING THE TRUTH

Ok! Let's suppose that nothing was lost in the translation process. Let's suppose the scribes didn't make deliberate changes. Let's even suppose the scribes made no big accidental errors. That still leaves one huge question unanswered. How do we know the original authors were telling the truth in the first place? Maybe Jesus' biographies are just well preserved lies.

In the following chapters I'll often refer to things Jesus is meant to have said or done. If Jesus never actually did these things, Christianity is nothing but a sick joke. So, how do you know they weren't making it all up?

The first thing to remember is that all four biographies are based on eye-witness accounts. Two of them (Luke and Mark) were written by men who personally knew or interviewed eye-witnesses. This would be like you interviewing me to write an essay on my wife, Buff. The other two (Matthew and John) appear to have been written by eye-witnesses themselves (although in Matthew's case this is less certain): men who travelled and worked with Jesus for over three years. This would be like *me* writing an essay on Buff.

The second thing to keep in mind is that many of the eyewitnesses (upon whom the biographies are based) were either imprisoned or executed for proclaiming what they'd seen. You've got to ask yourself: if it was a lie and they knew it, why did they die for it? It's one thing to die for something you truly believe in (heaps of people have done that) but it's another thing completely to die for something you know is false.

Imagine I came to you saying that I'd seen a UFO. Suppose it was illegal to make such claims and as a result I was thrown in prison until I retracted my statement. Add to this hundreds of other eyewitnesses, all claiming to have seen the same UFO, all thrown in prison, and after several months, all executed along with me, for our belief. What would you conclude?

At the very least, you would have to conclude that we all really believed we'd witnessed a UFO. The big problem you would then have is working out how on earth hundreds of normal, sane individuals came to believe such a thing. Was it drugs? Was it an optical illusion? Was it watching too many *X-Files* episodes? Whatever it was, it couldn't have been a lie. No one dies for a lie they *know* to be a lie.

When you come to Jesus' biographies you have a similar problem, only bigger. What caused these people to believe they'd seen Jesus teach, heal, die and then rise again? Could it have been a three-year-long optical illusion? If they had simply made the whole thing up, why did they bother dying for a lie? Even those who weren't imprisoned or killed for their claims still had to endure family ridicule, loss of jobs and many other forms of persecution.

At 15, I would not have accepted the Bible's picture of Jesus. Even though I'd never read it, I thought it was unreliable. I thought it must have been an ancient scam. At the same time, however, I was quite willing to accept the picture of Jesus presented in the B-grade Hollywood films. How embarrassing! Now, however, I'm quite sure it's the other way around. The real 'scams' about Jesus are the ones in some of the modern films, books and musicals about Jesus' life, not in the ancient biographies.

CHAPTER

3

STRANGER THAN FICTION

I **READ SOMEWHERE,** "Fact is stranger than fiction because we write fiction to suit ourselves". I think this is often the case. Stories that are invented for mass consumption are usually moulded to what the public wants to hear and is likely to believe. True stories on the other hand, are not invented for the public. They just happen, and because of this, are often more bizarre than anything you could make up. Here are a few very weird examples.

- In Italy for around $6245 you can buy ready-made coffins that have beepers, two-way speakers, a torch, a small oxygen tank, and a sensor to detect a person's heartbeat, just in case.
- To this day in Oklahoma, USA there is a law which forbids giving alcohol to fish.
- In Greenberry Hill, London, in 1641, three men were hanged for the murder of a local magistrate. By pure coincidence their surnames were Green, Berry and Hill.
- In the mid-1700s a Russian peasant named Feodor Vassilyev gave birth to 69 children. In 27 separate pregnancies she had 16 pairs of twins, seven sets of triplets, and four sets of quadruplets.
- In 1664, 1785, and 1860, passenger ferries sank while crossing the Menai strait off North Wales. Amazingly, each disaster occurred on December 5th. More bizarre than this, however, is that on all three occasions the name of the sole survivor was Hugh Williams.

Believe it or not, these stories are true. They are good evidence that 'fact is often stranger than fiction'. The birth of Jesus, recorded in the original biographies, is another bizarre example of this 'stranger than fiction' principle.

ENCOUNTER OF THE DIVINE KIND

Imagine you had to make up a story about God sending someone into the world to act as his ambassador; someone who was meant to show everyone what the Creator was like and how to get in touch with him (which is exactly what the biographies say of Jesus). How would *you* start the story? What sort of birth would *you* invent?

If it were up to me I would turn it into the biggest international event of history. For starters, it would take place in one of the major cities of the world; perhaps Los Angeles, since it'd be handy to have Hollywood on standby to turn it into a feature film. Just to be safe, I'd also make sure it occurred in the very best hospital in town, with all the best doctors present. The news crews of every major nation would be present, and the President of the USA would be invited to make a post-birth speech to the globe, welcoming God's ambassador to our planet. The whole thing would be beamed, via satellite, to all the cities of the world, and there could perhaps even be a live video-conference over the Internet. Quite simply, I would make it HUGE. It would make the alien invasion in the movie *Independence Day* look like a family picnic. After all, this is meant to be GOD'S ambassador. What ever else God is, he must be big.

Silly as all this sounds, I'm just trying to illustrate that if you or I were *inventing* a story about the birth of God's ambassador, we'd at least make sure it had an air of 'importance' about it, wouldn't we? When you read about the birth of Jesus, however, you get nothing like this. In fact, the reports of Jesus' birth are virtually the opposite of my version. Nothing you'd expect to happen, happened. And many things you'd never expect to happen, did. The reports are so strange, I find it difficult to believe the authors simply invented them for popular consumption. It's as if they didn't care whether we believed it or not; they were just reporting the facts, strange as they sound.

KID BORN IN SHED SAVES WORLD

Well then, what was so strange about the birth of Jesus? Put simply, there is very little in the story that is HUGE. Take for example where he is said to have been born. Here's part of the report, taken from Luke's biography:

Mary was engaged to Joseph and travelled with him to Bethlehem. She was soon going to have a baby, and while they were there, she gave birth to her firstborn son. She dressed him in baby clothes and laid him in a manger [an animal feeding trough], because there was no room for them in the inn.

This is odd! Jesus was not born in a large city like Los Angeles (or even Jerusalem) but in a little country town about 10 kms south of Jerusalem, called Bethlehem—a town about the size of Dunedoo (Where?? Exactly!). There was no fancy hospital, not even a trendy home birth. There wasn't even room in the local Bethlehem Pub. As a result, Jesus ended up being born in a barn, and then, instead of being laid down in a cot, he was put in a 'manger'—an animal feeding trough. I imagine Joseph and Mary would have given the trough a good clean first, but it's still a pretty rough way to come into the world, especially if you're meant to be God's ambassador, sent to show people what God is like.

Then there's the publicity; there was hardly any. And the little there was, was pretty lame if you ask me. Here's how Luke's account continues:

That night in the fields near Bethlehem some shepherds were guarding their sheep. All at once an angel came down to them from the Lord and said, "I have good news for you, which will make everyone happy. This very day in King David's home town a Saviour was born for you. He is Christ the Lord. You will know who he is, because you will find him dressed in baby clothes and lying in a manger". They hurried off and found Mary and Joseph, and they saw the baby lying in a manger. When the shepherds saw Jesus, they told his parents what the angel had said about him. Everyone listened and was surprised.

* By the way, all the quotes from the Bible can be tracked down using the Appendix on p.128.

Admittedly, the angels must have been quite spectacular, but they are not the focus of this scene. The people entrusted with publicising God's ambassador were shepherds, and they were quite unspectacular. I mean, being a sheep-minder (that's all shepherds did) was not exactly a high credibility job. Like I said before, if I were inventing a story about the birth of God's ambassador, I'd put some important officials at the scene, just to give it some credibility. The last people I'd leave the publicity to would be shepherds. It's no wonder people were "surprised" when they heard what these guys had to say.

If all this is true, this is a perfect example of fact being stranger than fiction. God's ambassador, born in a shed—how bizarre!

A GOD FOR LITTLE PEOPLE

Now, believe it or not, this strange beginning to Jesus' life is actually more significant than people often realise. If Jesus was God's ambassador—someone who is to show us what the Creator is like—this birth story tells us something amazing about what God must be like. Let me try and explain.

When I was first introduced to Christianity I had this idea that God was a big, powerful, great-grandfather-figure, who spoke in a deep, loud voice and took pleasure using his power to boss us little humans around. But then something dawned on me. If God planned for his own ambassador to be born in a tiny little town, then placed in an animal feeding trough with no one but common shepherds there to witness it, what must that say about God himself? Surely it means there must be more to God than POWER and SIZE and bossing people around. It means he must also be *humble*. It means he must have time for ordinary people. It means Jesus' visit to the planet is not just to tell us we're horrible creatures who'd better get our act together. His visit must be about getting his own hands dirty and getting alongside the little people. As we look at the rest of Jesus' life throughout this book we'll discover that this is precisely what happens.

The man who started Buddhism (Siddhartha Gautama) was a wealthy and powerful prince; the man who started Islam (Muhammad) was a renowned and fearsome warrior; but the man who started Christianity was born in a shed. He spent most of his life unknown, and ended up being executed as a criminal. At the very least, this tells us that the God Jesus represented (as ambassador) isn't out of reach or disinterested in our lives, but comes right up close. He isn't just interested in conquering the world like a grumpy old king (he could do that in a second if he wanted to) but in getting alongside it like a father or a friend.

The beginning of Jesus' life is very strange, not at all what you'd expect at the birth of God's ambassador. But, like I said, fact is often stranger than fiction. And, in a way, I'm glad about these strange, small beginnings, because it means that God may just have time for ordinary people, like us.

CHAPTER

4

THE STRANGEST FAN CLUB
IN THE WORLD

DANNY IS A BLOKE I met in a maximum security gaol a few years ago. I was there (voluntarily) performing with a band. After the concert, Danny came up to me and introduced himself. He told me that just two weeks before, a fellow inmate had asked for a Bible. Within an hour of receiving it, he was knifed by other prisoners. To my surprise, Danny was one of a small group of prisoners who, despite this sort of violence, were determined to make Jesus their top priority in life.

Miriam is an Aboriginal leader up in the Northern Territory. To this day she lives less than a kilometre from the tree she was born under. She's also one of our country's top Aboriginal painters. Strange thing is, most of her paintings use traditional aboriginal styles and symbols to describe how important *Jesus* is to her and her people.

Matthew was a member of Australia's top male stripper show. He had money, fame and all the sex he'd ever dreamt of. But a weird thing happened one day. He bumped into a nerdy class mate from his high school days in Queensland, who told him about the life of Jesus. That conversation turned Matt's life around. When I met Matt a few weeks later, he'd just quit the strip show and was starting out in a whole new direction. He too was determined to make Jesus his top priority.

Shashi grew up at the very top of Indian society. She's what you call 'Brahman' class. Her father was not only a wealthy businessman, he was also a Hindu leader and mentor to hundreds. In her teenage years, Shashi learnt about Jesus and she began to love what she learnt. For this she was ridiculed by the family, beaten up and forced to marry a strict Hindu man against her wishes. Despite all this, she remains to this day one of Jesus' biggest admirers.

Meeting people like Shashi and the others has taught me a valuable lesson. Once upon a time I would have thought that to be 'into Jesus' you had to be a do-gooding-middle-class-anglo-saxon-sandal-wearing-nerd; someone who was too dumb to believe anything other than what they were brought up to believe. The fact is, Danny, Miriam, Matt, Shashi, and millions of others like them, make this impression irrelevant. Jesus' life continues to have an impact on every sort of person you could imagine, including the sandal-wearing-nerds of the world. And what's more, this has always been the case.

THE SUPER STAR

Right from the beginning of Jesus' life, the most unlikely characters expressed deep interest in him. The shepherds mentioned in Luke's biography are one example, but a much better one is found in Matthew's biography. There we are told about a very odd bunch of visitors who turn up on Mary's doorstep asking to see her toddler.

The story I'm referring to is often called *The Three Wise Kings*. It features in many Christmas cards and carols, and some of the Jesus films as well. Unfortunately, most of the cards, carols and films get the story wrong. For starters, the visitors weren't kings, they were 'Magi', which means they were powerful ambassadors or political advisors for a foreign king. There weren't necessarily three of them either. There could have been 50 for all we know. Matthew didn't bother to tell us. Nor did they find Jesus at his birth, as is often portrayed. It was actually some months later. Jesus could have been as old as two when these visitors eventually found him.

One part of the story which the cards, carols and films do get right is how these Magi managed to find their way to Jesus. They apparently followed a star all the way from their homeland (which was probably where Iraq is today) to the town where Jesus was staying, 10km outside Jerusalem. This sounds a little too weird, doesn't it? Who has ever heard of following a star around the world? However, before we dismiss this as a fairy-tale, there's something we should know. Every 804 years a rare conjunction of Jupiter and Saturn occurs and it looks like a brilliant star. Modern astronomers, studying ancient astronomical records, have discovered that about 2000 years ago (right about the time Jesus was born) this rare conjunction strangely occurred three times in the same year.*

Don't get me wrong. I'm not saying the Magi *definitely* followed this conjunction (as far as I'm concerned, it is just as likely the star was a miraculous astronomical event sent by the Creator). I am simply saying that if you are skeptical about the idea of a weird star leading foreign ambassadors across the world, it's worth suspending that skepticism, since we know for a fact there was a very rare astronomical sight visible from that part of the world at just the right time.

---

* I got this from a Time magazine article, quoted in *Is the New Testament history?* by Paul Barnett, p. 122. (Hodder & Stoughton, 1994)

THE MULTICULTURAL KID

Imagine how weird this would have seemed to poor Mary, the mother of Jesus. There she is one day, looking after her little toddler, when a bunch of very, very weird looking foreigners knock on the door. "Hi, we're not from around here, but a star led us to your town and we believe your baby is God's ambassador. We'd like to worship him if that's OK with you." How would you react? If a bunch of strangers turned up on my doorstep wanting to see my baby, I can assure you they wouldn't get into the house. I'd probably slam the door and call the police. But Mary (who's slowly getting used to strange things happening around her son) invites these Magi in. Here's part of Matthew's biography:

> When the men went into the house and saw the child with Mary, his mother, they knelt down and worshipped him. They took out their gifts of gold, frankincense, and myrrh and gave them to him.

Picture this! A group of educated, powerful, wealthy, grown men get down on their hands and knees and worship a toddler. Not only that, they give the boy the type of gifts that, in the ancient world, were reserved for kings (frankincense and myrrh were expensive powders you could turn into incense and perfume). This is very unexpected.

The most unexpected part of this story, however, is not that these guys *worshipped* Jesus, it's that *these guys* worshipped Jesus. Magi were what you might call 'pagans'. They belonged to a completely different religion, race and culture from that of Joseph, Mary, Jesus and the rest of downtown Bethlehem. In those days, a Jewish girl like Mary was forbidden to even talk with such 'outsiders', let alone have them under her roof or, even worse, have 'religious' contact with them. But Mary must have understood something about her son that many people, even today, fail to realise—his life was destined to have an impact on every type of person you could imagine. She must have known she could never keep her son to herself. This little toddler had international, multicultural significance. Put another way, the visit of these mysterious foreigners was a sign that Jesus' fan club was *not* going to be a closed one. Membership was going to be open to everyone, no matter what their racial, religious, social, or even moral, background.

The day I met Miriam (the aboriginal lady I mentioned earlier) and heard her speak about her faith in Jesus, I couldn't help thinking how amazing it was that a man born in a shed on the other side of the world 2000 years ago could have such a significant impact on the life of a traditional aboriginal woman all these years later. It's just not the sort of thing I would have predicted. According to Matthew's biography, however, Miriam's devotion to Jesus is exactly the sort of thing I should have expected. Ever since those mysterious Magi first worshipped Jesus all those years ago, Jesus' fan club has included some of the most unlikely members. Who knows, perhaps you're one of them.

THE GLORY DAYS

"Sports hero, rock star, royalty and guru, all rolled into one – that's how the masses treated him … for a while anyhow."

CHAPTER

5

JESUS AND ARNIE

I MENTIONED EARLIER THAT one of the reasons I avoided taking Jesus seriously for so long was the impression that he was weak. As a young Aussie bloke, 'strength' and 'power' were important qualities for me. My hero was more likely to be someone like Arnold Schwarzenegger in the *Terminator* films than the Jesus of the Hollywood films. The thought that Jesus walked around in robes talking about 'love' and 'peace' all the time was not a strong draw card. The few things I had heard of Jesus' teaching only confirmed this impression.

He apparently said things like "If someone hits you on the right cheek let them hit you on the left as well". As a budding martial artist, this seemed ridiculous. He also said, "Blessed are the meek". As far as I was concerned "meek" meant weak. And then there was all that stuff about "becoming like a little child". I had reached puberty! There was no way I was going to retreat back into childhood!

However, it didn't take much for this impression to be shown up as fake. The day I started reading the biographies of Jesus' life for myself I instantly discovered that 'weak' is just about the last thing you could call Jesus.

THE BUSH-TUCKER MAN

Take Mark's biography for example. In the first couple of paragraphs of the book, you meet a man called John the Baptist. This guy lived in the outback. He was a rough-as-guts 'bush-man'. He apparently wore clothes made out of camels' hair and lived on desert food–grasshoppers and honey, mostly. This guy was the original bush-tucker man. Anyway, people would make day trips out to the desert where John lived just to hear him give speeches. What is fascinating about this man is that most of his speeches were about Jesus. By this stage Jesus was grown up; about 30 years old. And just months before Jesus started his public career, this is what John the Baptist was saying about him, according to Mark's biography:

> John also told the people, "Someone more powerful is going to come. And I'm not good enough even to stoop down and untie his sandals".

Here is this 'tough as nails' outback-man, admitting that Jesus is so powerful he didn't even feel worthy enough to undo his shoes (which is what a slave would normally do for a master). This makes my impression of Jesus as a 'Nancy-boy' look pretty lame.

Sure enough, in a matter of months Jesus burst onto the public stage, and everything John 'Bush-Man' Baptist had said about him was undeniably true. Jesus' power and leadership took everyone by surprise.

PROFESSOR CHRIST

From the moment he opened his mouth, Jesus showed incredible power as a teacher. This may sound like an odd thing to say. Whoever thought of describing their Maths teacher or Biology lecturer as 'powerful'? But Jesus didn't teach subjects like Maths and Science (obviously). He taught about the GIANT issues of life, like death, sex, money, violence, God, crime, the end of the world, and stuff like that. And when he went around giving speeches on these topics, people could hardly believe their ears. Here is how Mark's biography describes it:

> **Jesus went into the Jewish meeting place and started teaching. Everyone was amazed at his teaching. He taught with authority, and not like the teachers of the Law of Moses.**

The most amazing thing about this brief comment is the comparison between Jesus and the current teachers of his day. The guys called 'teachers of the Law of Moses' were no dummies. They spent their whole lives doing nothing but studying and lecturing. Their knowledge of Jewish literature, language, history, philosophy and religion was vast. They were literally the university professors of ancient Israel. And yet, here is this 30 year-old carpenter who opens his mouth and makes the academics look as though they have no authority. As the story of Jesus' life unfolds, the jealousy of these religious and academic professionals has a lot to do with Jesus' arrest, trial and execution. That's how threatening his authority as a teacher became.

JESUS AND THE EXORCIST

Jesus also displayed incredible power over evil. Unfortunately, it's impossible to raise a subject like exorcism without thinking of films like *The Exorcist* or the TV show *The X-Files*. In these shows, 'evil spirits' are glamourised and Hollywood-ised into *unbelievability*. Demons are able to make their victims' heads spin 360 degrees around, cause them to throw-up green vomit and make sharp objects fly down hallways and chase petrified priests out of the house. I saw an *X-Files* episode recently that was almost exactly like this. The biographies of Jesus' life, however, have no such glamourisation. They do speak of personal, dark forces called "evil spirits" that can infect people's lives, but they are so 'matter-of-fact' about it, it is hard to see any similarity between them and the Hollywood versions.

It is tempting to dismiss any talk of 'spirits' as a load of pre-scientific nonsense—the sort of thing 'simple' people believed before we discovered medical explanations for human sicknesses. The problem with this argument is that Jesus' biographies also speak of purely physical sickness, without any mention of a spiritual dimension. Jesus is said to have healed these as well. Perhaps the truer criticism is not that the ancient Middle East 'spiritualised' everything, but that we in the modern Western world have tried to 'naturalise' everything!

Anyway, all four biographies are adamant—there are dark, personal beings called 'evil spirits', and Jesus displayed absolute power over them. To quote Mark's biography again:

> Suddenly a man with an evil spirit in him entered the meeting place and yelled, "Jesus from Nazareth, what do you want with us? Have you come to destroy us? I know who you are! You are God's Holy One".
>
> Jesus told the evil spirit, "Be quiet and come out of the man!"
>
> The spirit shook him. Then it gave a loud shout and left. Everyone was completely surprised and kept saying to each other, "What is this? Even the evil spirits obey him". News about Jesus quickly spread ...

In *The Exorcist* and other demon possession movies, the priest doing the so-called 'exorcism' splashes holy water over everything, says long drawn-out prayers and waves a wooden cross around. This usually goes on for hours, and even then, if the priest wins, he only just does so. Mark's biography couldn't be more different. Jesus says one sentence and it's over—no fuss, and no flying objects. Everyone in the meeting is amazed. Jesus' power extends even over the darkest of evil forces.

JESUS AND THE ENVIRONMENT

A third way Jesus demonstrated power was over nature itself. There are some bizarre stories recorded in the biographies which show that even the environment was under Jesus' control. Here is a classic example, recorded in Mark's account:

> Jesus' disciples started across the lake with him in the boat. Some other boats followed along. Suddenly a strong wind struck the lake. Waves started splashing into the boat, and it was about to sink.
>
> Jesus was in the back of the boat with his head on a pillow, and he was asleep.
>
> His disciples woke him and said, "Teacher, don't you care that we're about to drown?"

We need to appreciate that a number of Jesus' friends were professional fishermen (or anglers as they like to be known now). These men knew the sea, and they knew storms, so it must have been some storm to get them worried for their lives! And yet, at the same time, Jesus is asleep. I think that's quite funny. Professional anglers are scared to death of drowning, and Jesus the carpenter is having a quiet nap.

What happens then, however, is anything but funny.

> Jesus got up and ordered the wind and the waves to be quiet. The wind stopped, and everything went calm.

I've tried this. On about my third attempt at sailboarding, I got stuck in a serious storm out in the middle of Sydney Harbour. I did all the commanding and praying (and swearing) I could think of. There was absolutely no change in the weather believe me! I eventually had to pull the sail down and paddle nervously back to shore, being careful to avoid the frequent ferries. Not so with Jesus. He stands up in the middle of a raging storm and tells it to be quiet, and it does what it's told! If you were there that day and saw this with your own eyes, how would you have reacted? What impression would this man have had on you? Here is how the Apostles reacted:

Now they were more afraid than ever, and said to each other, "Who is this? Even the wind and the waves obey him!"

When you think of Jesus, I bet 'fearsome' is not one of the first things that comes to mind. But it's exactly how those who knew him thought of him. The 'Hollywood Jesus' may have looked like a *woos*, but the real Jesus made grown men scared—as Mark's biography puts it, "more afraid than ever". One minute they're afraid of drowning; next minute they're afraid of the man who saved them. And it wasn't the last time Jesus frightened them like this either.

I've got to confess, I'm a little embarrassed that I ever thought Jesus was a wimp. Nowadays, I read about Jesus' life and think, "Who needs Arnie as a hero?"

CHAPTER

6

IN THE EVENT OF AN
EMERGENCY...

BRITISH AIRWAYS FLIGHT 009 was bound for Australia from Indonesia several years ago. Suddenly, 10 kilometres above the Indian Ocean, the Boeing 747 began to free-fall. The passengers were alerted by the captain, "Ladies and Gentleman, this is your captain speaking. We have a small problem. All four engines have stopped. We are doing our damnedest to get them going again. I trust you are not in too much distress".

Well, "distress" was an understatement. Everyone, including the crew and captain, knew they were going to crash.

People who had never prayed in their life began to do so. Others sat in frozen silence. Strangers held hands. Husbands and wives said their goodbyes. Mothers clung to their children.

One passenger's reaction, however, was quite amazing. Charles Capewell and his son noticed smoke throughout the cabin. The son then looked out the window and noticed what looked like flames pouring out of the engines. He said to his father, "Dad, the engine's on fire!". Charles responded, "Well, you'd better pull the blind down and pretend it's not happening". That's exactly what they did!

TOTAL! FINAL! UNSTOPPABLE!

When I first read this, I thought, "How bizarre! You're about to crash into the Indian Ocean and all you can think of doing is pulling the blind down and pretending it's not happening!" But then I realised, that's not so unusual after all. In fact, this is precisely what many of us do when it comes to the topic of death. In our own way, we refuse to think about it. It's as if we believe that avoiding the issue will make it go away. We sort of close the blind and pretend it won't happen.

The problem, of course, is that it will happen. Death is just about the only certain thing in life. There is nothing so sure, and powerful, and deadly, as death! It is the ultimate, unstoppable enemy of humanity. Nothing any of us can do will make it disappear. Those of you who have lost a loved one will know exactly what I mean.

One of the overwhelming things about the death of someone you're close to is the sense that this separation from your friend or family member is 'total' and 'final'. This sensation often first hits you at the funeral. It suddenly dawns on you that you will never see this person again. You will never speak to them, laugh with them, eat with them, argue with them, or even touch them, again.

Jesus was not immune to this sense of 'loss' either. There is an occasion recorded in John's biography when Jesus learns about the death of one of his closest friends, a man named Lazarus. It is an astonishing story in many respects, and what it tells us about Jesus and his view of death is extremely valuable.

Jesus is in the middle of one of his extensive tours. He has been speaking to thousands of people, all of whom are desperate to get close to him, to hear his words and watch his miracles. Out of the blue, Jesus receives word that his good friend is very ill. Jesus somehow knew that Lazarus was more than sick, and sure enough, when he arrived at his home town several days later, Lazarus had been dead for four days. Here's part of John's biography:

> When Jesus got to Bethany, he found that Lazarus had already been in the tomb for four days. Bethany was only about three kilometres from Jerusalem, and many people had come from the city to comfort Martha and Mary because their brother had died.

Martha and Mary, Lazarus' sisters, were also close friends of Jesus. When they heard that he had arrived they ran to meet him. If anyone had answers about death and the afterlife, it had to be Jesus, they thought. The biography continues:

> Mary went to where Jesus was. Then as soon as she saw him, she knelt at his feet and said, "Lord, if you'd been here, my brother wouldn't have died".

> When Jesus saw that Mary and the people with her were crying, he was terribly upset and asked, "Where have you put his body?" They replied, "Lord, come and you'll see".

> Jesus started crying, and the people said, "See how much he loved Lazarus".

This is a very different picture of Jesus from the one captured in many of the Hollywood films. The movies often present Jesus as cool, calm and collected. He never laughs. He never cries. He just remains the same; a bit like a zombie. But here, at the funeral of one of his closest friends, Jesus could not hold back the tears. Jesus, just like you and me, understood the awful totality and finality of death.

PARTIAL! TEMPORARY! STOPPED!

The story does not end here, however. What happened then is unbeliev-able (so to speak)! Jesus stood outside the tomb—a small cave with a huge boulder rolled across the entrance—and ordered some men to roll away the stone. Martha saw what Jesus was doing and responded:

"Lord, you know that Lazarus has been dead for four days, and there will be a bad smell."

Bad smell or not, Jesus insisted the tomb be opened, and the men obeyed (as you would when this man asked you to do something). Jesus prayed, and then shouted what must have sounded like madness to everyone else at the funeral. Here's how John's biography reports it:

When Jesus had finished praying, he shouted, "Lazarus, come out!"

To me, this sounds like an outrageous thing to say at your best friend's funeral. I've been to a few funerals for friends and I can assure you, if someone had stood up and shouted "come out" at my mate's coffin, I would not have appreciated it. You'd have to think it was either a sick joke, or else the person was delirious with grief. That's unless, of course, that person was Jesus. The people at this funeral knew Jesus had healed people of sickness. They may have even heard about the violent storm he had silenced. For the few seconds after Jesus shouted these words, I'm sure people paused in a state of shock, disbelief and partial expectation. Could Jesus have mastery over the greatest of all powers—death? Could Jesus outdo the seemingly overwhelming totality and finality of death?

John's biography continues without any glamourisation or hype:

The man who had been dead came out. His hands and feet were wrapped with strips of burial cloth, and a cloth covered his face. Jesus then told the people, "Untie him and let him go".

As scientifically impossible as this sounds, Jesus raised a man from the dead. This is not a 'near death' experience, like the ones we read about in some modern medical books. This is a "four-days-dead-as-a-dodo-then-back-again" experience.

Now, we need to be careful we don't dismiss this account as a story written *by* and *for* 'simple people' who easily believed in magic and miracles. This is simply *not* the case. Jewish people then (as now) were an intensely practical bunch of people. On the whole, Judaism is a very *un*miraculous religion. In Jesus' day there were two views about the 'afterlife'. One insisted there is nothing after death—you just rot in the ground. The other insisted that the only 'rising from the dead' you can expect is something God himself will do at the very end of history—on Judgement Day. In fact, Jesus himself taught this. But no one in Jesus' day was *inclined* to believe that a dead person could be brought back to life in the way Lazarus had been. As Jews, they would have been very skeptical about such an idea. That is, until the day Jesus attended Lazarus' funeral. That day, everyone had all the evidence they needed to understand that there was one man who could outdo death, who's power and authority extended even to the enemy of all enemies. Jesus had out-mastered death itself.

A SERIOUS PROMISE

The account of Lazarus' funeral doesn't just tell us about Jesus' incredible power and authority over death. It also tells us something about our own death. I didn't mention earlier that Jesus used his friend's funeral as an opportunity to teach people about what happens after death. Raising Lazarus was the ultimate proof that what Jesus thought and taught about death is most likely true. Here's part of the material Jesus delivered that day:

"I am the one who raises the dead to life! Everyone who has faith in me will live, even if they die. And everyone who lives because of faith in me will never really die."

Jesus did not believe we just rot in the ground when we die. He did not believe we are reincarnated into another existence either. He insisted that beyond the grave there was life, and that he was the one who could assure us a place in that life. What Jesus did for Lazarus was a brief demonstration of what Jesus will one day do for "everyone who has faith in him". Trust in him and you can be sure that your death will not be total or final. That is what Jesus said, time and time again.

British Airways flight 009 had a lucky escape. The pilot did one last restart and, out of the blue, all the engines amazingly sprang back to life. But this kind of fairytale ending is pretty rare.

Years ago a plane left from Bombay Airport, India. Within minutes of take-off, one of the engines caught on fire. The plane lost power and fell to the ground. Everyone on board was killed. My dad was in Bombay at the time, so when Mum heard about the crash on the news, she was worried. The plane that went down wasn't the one Dad was meant to be on, but mum knew he hated waiting in airports, and it would have been just like him to wangle his way onto the first available plane. That night, while my brothers and I were watching TV, the phone rang. It was a call from India. Our dad was killed in the crash.

It's hard to describe what I felt in those first few weeks after losing Dad. But one of the things I remember thinking was just how *absolute* death seemed. There was no way to pull the blind down and pretend it wouldn't happen. It was the one thing in life I was never going to avoid, or master, or even come to grips with. It was going to win every time.

Years later, when I started to read the biographies of Jesus' life, I stumbled across this account of Lazarus' funeral. There I saw a different picture of death. There I saw that there was one man who could outdo this great enemy, whose power and authority ruled even over death itself. And there I read of a promise Jesus made that day; a promise I can't help thinking he will fulfill:

"I am the one who raises the dead to life! Everyone who has faith in me will live, even if they die."

CHAPTER

7

MEETING THE MEGASTAR

IF YOU'D ASKED ME at 16 who I'd like to meet more than anyone else in the world, I would have said, "Bono from U2", for sure. But how on earth do you meet the lead singer of one of the biggest rock bands in the world? These guys apparently earn $200 a minute, each. Why on earth would they bother with a starry-eyed teenager just starting out in his first band? When they toured Australia I tried ringing the 5-star hotel they were staying at and saying that I was the 'brother' of the Edge (guitarist)—I had heard that they were Christians so I figured I wasn't *exactly* lying. The lady at the desk politely hung up on me.

Then one of my friends had an idea. She suggested we dress up, go to the hotel and hang around in the lobby as if we were hotel guests. So that's what I did. The next day, a friend and I dressed up in a suit and tie, got ourselves a briefcase and caught a taxi straight to the hotel door. To our surprise the doorman opened the door, and showed us straight into the hotel, right past the U2 fans who were banned from entering. We hung around in one of the hotel shops until, sure enough, the Edge and Larry Mullen Jr (drummer) walked out of the lift toward us. We pounced on them and spent the next five or ten minutes getting things signed, taking photos and asking countless questions. We were wrapped. So wrapped we went straight home, told our mates, and organised another attempt for the following day.

The next day, about eight of us dressed up in suits, got briefcases and caught taxis in convoy to the hotel. The same thing happened. The doorman opened the door and showed us straight past a bunch of very suspicious U2 fans, right into the hotel. This time we headed for the restaurant. There we ordered toast and bottomless coffee. We must have hung around in that place for three hours, waiting for the band to arrive for breaky. At about 11:30am Bono arrived and sat at a table right near us. I left him alone with his breakfast partner for about 10 minutes and then introduced myself and asked if he had the time to meet my mates. He said he'd love to, just as soon as he finished recording the interview he was in the middle of. I looked down and there on the table was a recorder, still recording…Oops! About 15 minutes later he came over to our table and chatted and signed all the stuff we had managed to cram into our briefcases. It was great!

About 10 minutes later, as I finished about my fifth coffee for the morning, the hotel manager walked over to our table. We braced ourselves and got ready to be thrown out. He looked at us and said, "Lads, I know exactly what you've been doing all morning. I like your initiative. Stay as long as you like". We couldn't believe our ears. We were so happy we bought another round of toast and coffee. When we finally left, all the other U2 fans outside the hotel yelled abuse at us and made all sorts of interesting finger signs, but I didn't mind—I had met the guys from U2.

A MEMORABLE ENTRANCE

People have always done ridiculous things to get the attention of famous people; things you'd never dream of doing to meet a 'normal' person. With Jesus, it was no different. It's easy to forget that in his time Jesus was as popular as an individual could get. No one drew the crowds he drew. On one occasion well over 5000 men (not even counting women and children) gathered to hear him. Admittedly, Gillian Anderson (from *The X-Files*) drew a crowd of 10 000 at a recent in-store appearance, but her fans only had to go to their local shopping centre. Jesus' admirers often had to travel out into the countryside, on foot, just to get to hear him.

On one occasion, Jesus was in his home town as part of his speaking tour. Arrangements had been made for him to make an appearance at someone's home. Some of these ancient homes were huge, open buildings that could accommodate large crowds for parties and special occasions. In Mark's biography we're told that Jesus once again packed out the venue. In fact,

So many gathered that there was no room left, not even outside the door...

How about that? There wasn't even room left *outside* the venue.

What happens then is truly amazing. A bunch of friends bring their disabled mate to the venue to meet Jesus. They must have heard about his ability to heal people, and thought now was their big chance. Unfortunately, the crowd was so huge they couldn't even see Jesus, let alone get close enough to grab his attention. Then one of them thought of a plan. They climbed up the side of the building onto the roof. Once there, they began to dig a hole through the ceiling. Ancient roofs were made of mud, wood and branches, not tin or tiles like ours, so it wouldn't have been *too* difficult—just very rude. They then hoisted their friend up onto the roof and with the help of ropes attached to a stretcher, they lowered him through the ceiling, right into the middle of the crowd.

Imagine being inside the house. There you are, listening to Jesus give a speech, and all of a sudden a hole starts to appear in the ceiling—a huge hole. Then out of the hole you see a man on a stretcher being lowered to the floor, right in front of the guest speaker. It's outrageous—far more outrageous than my U2 adventure.

I suspect the crowd were pretty annoyed at the way these men weaselled their way into the venue and stole Jesus' attention. I guess the owner of the house would have been especially disturbed. After all, they had taken his roof apart. I very much doubt he said to them, "I like your initiative. Stay as long as you like". Anyway, whatever the crowd or the owner of the house thought, Jesus was impressed. To him, this outrageous entrance was not rudeness, but a display of their great confidence in him. They were convinced Jesus could meet their deep need, and were willing to do whatever it took to get close to him. This sort of 'faith' (as the biographies call it) always got a good response from Jesus. And this occasion is no exception. Jesus was so impressed, he interrupted his own speech and gave his full attention to the needs of this man. Here's how Mark's biography puts it:

When Jesus saw how much faith they had, he said to the crippled man, "My friend, your sins are forgiven".

If I was that crippled guy (or one of his friends), I'm not sure I'd be very happy with these words. After all the trouble I'd gone to, why on earth didn't Jesus do the obvious thing and heal me? Why would he say, "Your sins are forgiven", when it's perfectly clear what I've come for?

SMALL WORD, BIG PROBLEM

The answer to that question takes us to the heart of what Jesus was on about in his career. Although Jesus was concerned about the great variety of problems in his world—physical disabilities, loneliness, poverty, inequality—he was adamant that there was one, much bigger, problem. He insisted that men and women had put God offside by the way they lived their lives. Whether by simply ignoring God or consciously rejecting him, according to Jesus, we have annoyed the Creator of the universe! That's one hell of a problem (literally) if you ask me.

Jesus' word for this problem was 'sin'. This is a very unpopular word these days. In fact, just the other night I saw Wendy Matthews and

Christine Anu sing a duet version of an old black Gospel song called 'Oh Happy Day'. The chorus of the song goes, "Oh happy day, when Jesus washed my sins away". But Wendy and Christine's version mysteriously lost that unfashionable little word. Their chorus sang, "Oh happy day, when Jesus washed my *fears* away". It's quite easy to change a classic Gospel song I guess, but it's not so easy when you look at Jesus' biographies. Jesus seemed quite serious about the word. To him, it summed up the most serious problem in the human race.

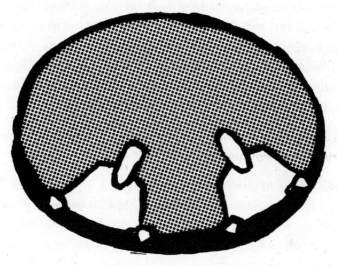

If the deepest need in our society is for *employment,* politicians are probably the most important people in the world. If *education* is what we need, academics are our saviours. If we need *stress relief or mental health,* then psychologists are the gurus of the 90s. If *spiritual enlightenment* is the most profound human need, then my local New Age bookshop owner would have to be the woman of the moment.

But what if Jesus is right? What if we have wronged God and need his forgiveness? If that's true, it kind of makes the need for 'stress relief' look pretty lame. I mean, if God is going to hold my wrong thoughts and actions against me, it doesn't matter how stress-relieved, employed, educated or enlightened I feel—I'm in trouble!

If Jesus is right about the importance of 'sin', then what he said to the disabled man that day makes perfect sense. He wasn't ignoring this man's need, he was simply redirecting his attention to a greater need. The man may have come for physical healing but he ended up getting a much better deal than that. His sins were forgiven.

WHO DOES JESUS THINK HE IS?

Now, of course, this raises a huge question. What on earth is *Jesus* doing handing out *God's* forgiveness? If you steal my guitar and then later apologise, it's up to me to decide to forgive you, not someone else. Suppose you did steal from me, then said sorry, and one of my friends standing by said, "Oh, that's OK. I forgive you". You'd be surprised wouldn't you? I'd be dumbfounded! If you've offended me, what right has anyone else got to hand out my forgiveness?

So, what is Jesus doing saying, "Your sins are forgiven"? Who on earth does he think he is? The crowd picks up on this, especially the professors of religion who were sitting there that day listening to Jesus. Here is their reaction:

> **Some of the teachers of the Law of Moses were sitting there. They started wondering, "Why would he say such a thing? He must think he is God! Only God can forgive sins".**

Jesus had some quick thinking to do. In those days, claiming to be God, or someone close to him, was a very serious crime. Nowadays, they just send men in white coats to take you away to a padded hospital room. In Jesus' day, you could be executed for it! Now, if I were Jesus, I would have backed down, saying, "I didn't mean I could forgive you. I meant God forgives you and I'd just like to pass on the good news". But Jesus didn't say anything like this. Mark's biography continues:

> **Straight away, Jesus knew what they were thinking, and he said, "Why are you thinking such things...I will show you that the Son of Man [a title Jesus often used of himself] has the right to forgive sins here on earth". So Jesus said to the man, "Get up! Pick up your mat and go on home".**

> **The man got straight up. He picked up his mat and went out while everyone watched in amazement. They praised God and said, "We've never seen anything like this!"**

Instead of backing down from his claim to forgive sins, Jesus gives a demonstration of his authority. He turns to the crippled man and asks him to stand up and walk home. And it works! The man gets to his feet, picks up his stretcher, and walks on out of there. Not only is this very nice of Jesus, it is also proof that he is able to hand out God's pardon. By meeting this man's obvious, physical need, Jesus was demonstrating that he has the power to meet the less obvious (though more serious) need. It certainly convinced the crowd, who sat there completely dumbfounded saying, "We've never seen anything like this!"

Out-teaching the intellectual elite of his society was impressive. Dispelling evil spirits with a single command was amazing. Controlling the physical environment was staggering. But what Jesus did this day is almost impossible to fathom. With all the authority of God himself, Jesus apparently wiped clean a man's whole life. He pronounced an 'INNOCENT' verdict over this man's life record. Whatever that guy had done wrong, Jesus forgave. And he did so with God's authority.

I don't know about you, but this puts a whole new spin on my idea of Jesus. I might have been able to dismiss Jesus' miracles as the work of a magician. But if it's true that Jesus has the authority to hand out God's forgiveness, that puts him in a whole new league. That puts him so close to God it's not funny.

If people were desperate to meet Jesus before the day he gave God's forgiveness to that crippled man, imagine the reaction afterwards. If people flocked to him (like my mates and I flocked to meet U2) because he could teach, heal and calm storms, imagine the hype when it got out that he had the right to give people a clean slate in life. Everyone wanted to meet him— politicians, children, peasants, soldiers, priests, criminals, kings, everyone. The crippled man's confidence in Jesus was soon expressed by hundreds, then thousands, of people. He soon became the unrivalled Megastar of his time, and for good reason, I think. People longed to hear him say to them, "Friend, your sins are forgiven".

CHAPTER

8

WHAT WOULD JESUS SAY TO MADONNA?

YOU MAY HAVE HEARD about the famous Madonna appearance on 'The David Letterman Show' in the USA. It was reported on news programs around the world. Once again, Madonna managed to shock the world with her radical approach to life. If you didn't catch the show it went like this:

Letterman introduced his famous guest saying,

> *"Our first guest tonight is one of the biggest stars in the world. In the past ten years she has sold over 80 million albums, starred in countless films, and slept with some of the biggest names in the entertainment industry."*

With an intro like that you knew this was going to be an interesting segment.

Out strutted Madonna, Cuban cigar in one hand, and her underwear in the other. Yes, her undies! They were her 'gift' to Letterman. Within seconds of her entrance Madonna turned on Letterman, swearing and insulting him, on live international TV:

> *"Incidently, you are a sick @#$% ... I don't know why I get so much &^%$#@ ...You're twisted", Madonna blurted.*

> *"You realise this is being broadcast, don't you?" replied a very nervous Letterman.*

Madonna did realise. She was counting on it. Throughout the rest of the interview she repeatedly swore, made crude jokes, and demanded that things go her way. At one stage she even screwed up the 'Top 10 List' (a regular feature of the show). Letterman, meanwhile, was trying to keep things rolling, conscious that millions of people were watching. When he tried to throw to a commercial break however, Madonna insisted,

> *"No! I don't think we should ever cut to a commercial. Let's keep talking and film every second of it."*

Madonna stayed on the show for three entire segments. She wouldn't leave—literally. Even though Counting Crows were out the back, waiting to perform, Madonna just kept things going her way. She didn't even take the hint when an audience member yelled, "Get off!" She wanted the whole show to herself. She didn't care about the rules. She's not a 'rules' kind of lady. In fact, at one point she summed up her view of things very well. She looked at Letterman and said, "I think we should break the rules".

Over the years Madonna has come to symbolise the Rule-Breaker. I'm not sure whether she planned it this way, or even if it is a fair judgement of her personal life, but it is certainly the popular perception of her among the record, TV, and film industries, not to mention the general public. Anyway, all this got me wondering what Jesus would say to a person like Madonna. Many religious people over the years have had their say about her, mostly pointing the finger and wanting her banned, but what would the man who started the Christian faith say if he were to meet her?

A 1ST CENTURY MADONNA

Fortunately, there's a brilliant moment in Jesus' life when he met a woman who was probably not too different from Madonna. She may not have been as famous, but in her home town she certainly had quite a 'reputation'. We are introduced to her in Luke's biography as "a sinful woman in that town". We're not told exactly what 'sinful woman' means, but let's just say it probably means she 'got around' a bit, and broke a few rules along the way.

What is amazing is that when Jesus visits this woman's home-town on one of his many tours, she is desperate to meet him. A 'rule-breaker' wants to meet the most famous religious leader of all time. That is odd! Most rule-breakers run a mile when religious people are around. I can remember a rebellious stage in my own life when I used to go to church (mainly out of guilt) but run out as soon as it finished so that no Christians could get their hands on me and make me feel even more guilty. But for this 'sinful woman' it's different. Perhaps she had heard something about Jesus that gave her an inkling that he was not like the religious bigots in her town.

But this lady has a large problem. Jesus is in the middle of a dinner party at the home of one of those religious bigots—a prominent religious leader, named Simon. Simon was a Pharisee, which means he was about as moral and religious as you could get in the 1st century. He was virtually the opposite of the sinful woman. She had a reputation as a rule-*breaker*, but Simon had a reputation as a rule-*keeper*. You just don't gatecrash a religious dinner party, especially if you're 'known' in the way this lady was.

But this is one very gutsy woman. She finds Simon's house, walks through the front door, down the hall, and right into the dining room. If that wasn't bad enough, she walks right over to Jesus and, in front of all these important guests, falls at his feet, and weeps. That is probably hard to imagine if you're thinking of a modern dining room table. (I mean, how did she fall at Jesus' feet? Did she crawl under the table or something?) In many Middle Eastern countries, you eat lying down on cushions around a low table. The guests lie on their left side with their head near the table, and eat with their right hand. Their feet (fortunately) are nowhere near the table. Falling at Jesus' feet would have been quite easy, just very rude.

Then, perhaps out of embarrassment that she has cried all over this great man's feet, she takes her hair out of her veil (something Middle Eastern women never did) and quickly wipes his feet dry with it. Then she begins kissing his feet and pouring expensive perfume all over them. Can you imagine how shocking this must have seemed? She might not have had as big an audience as Madonna had, but you can be sure this sinful woman caused just as big an outrage as Madonna did on that Letterman show.

JESUS VS RELIGION

The guests were furious, especially Simon. Simon had invited Jesus into his home, thinking he was a great religious teacher. But the way Jesus let this 'sinful woman' touch him and slobber all over him, completely destroyed Jesus' credibility. Here's what Simon mumbled to himself, according to Luke's biography:

> **"If this man really was a Prophet, he would know what kind of woman is touching him! He would know that she is a sinner."**

Simon wanted this woman publicly humiliated. After all, she had made her rule-breaking public, so why shouldn't she now be openly condemned? This would be the perfect time for Jesus to prove himself a great moral leader.

But Jesus will not do it!

Instead, what Jesus then does is very impressive. In front of all these stuffy religious guests, Jesus defends the gate-crashing, rule-breaking woman and rebukes his rule-keeping host. You should read Jesus' words for yourself. With this woman still at his feet, Jesus told Simon a story designed to make him understand the woman's actions, and face up to himself:

> **Jesus told him, "Two people were in debt to a moneylender [bank manager]. One of them owed him 500 silver coins [= $50,000], and the other owed him 50 [= $5,000]. Since neither of them could pay him back, the moneylender said that they didn't have to pay him anything. Which one of them will like him more?"**
>
> **Simon answered, "I suppose it would be the one who had owed more and didn't have to pay it back".**

As soon as Simon gives this answer, Jesus goes for the jugular (so to speak)! What he says is so daring that only Jesus could get away with it. He praises the woman's hospitality (even though she was uninvited) and accuses Simon of being a hopeless host. Here are Jesus' words:

> **"When I came into your home, you didn't give me any water so I could wash my feet [a normal Middle Eastern custom]. But she has washed my feet with her tears and dried them with her hair. You didn't greet me with a kiss [another custom of the day], but from the time I came in, she has not stopped kissing my feet. You didn't even pour olive oil on my head [an ancient way to freshen up], but she has poured perfume on my feet."**

This woman's outrageous actions that evening were not rudeness, as Simon thought, but appreciation. She knew she had stacked up a lot of debt with God (done a lot of things wrong, in other words), but she saw in Jesus the possibility of forgiveness. Jesus' story to Simon was a way of saying, "Look you religious bigot, this woman may have a bigger debt than you but at least she wants it cancelled. Her affection is a sign of her thankfulness to me that I can forgive her many wrongs".

Simon, on the other hand, seemed to have no sense of needing God's forgiveness. He seems to think he has no debt with God. As a result, he has no appreciation of Jesus. He sees Jesus as a moral enforcer, not as the one who has God's authority to forgive people for being immoral. But Simon is dead wrong. The two people in Jesus' story may have had different sized debts but, according to Jesus, neither of them could pay the bank manager back. In other words, Simon may have lived a more 'moral' life than the 'sinful woman', but he had still broken God's instructions and needed his forgiveness.

A FRESH START

Jesus then turns his attention away from the Pharisee. Jesus' concern is with the woman. He turns to her, forgetting about the rest of the dumbfounded guests, and says some quite beautiful words:

Then Jesus said to the woman, "Your sins are forgiven ... Because of your faith, you are now saved. May God give you peace!"

Imagine for a second what this would have felt like for the woman. She would have been used to feeling guilty and shameful. She would have been used to men like Simon pointing the finger at her and condemning her. But here was a man who didn't throw the rule book at her, but instead made her an amazing promise—her sins (wrong actions) were now forgiven. Her debt with God, even though it was large, was cancelled. Jesus offered her another go at life—a completely fresh start. And you can bet she took it!

So, what *would* Jesus say to Madonna? Well, it depends. If Madonna treated Jesus the way she treated Letterman, I don't think it would go down too well. But if Madonna, like this woman, came to Jesus looking for his acceptance, friendship and forgiveness, you can be dead sure what Jesus would say. Despite the finger-pointing and rule-book-throwing some of us might want to do, Jesus would say, "Your sins are forgiven". He would offer her a brand new start—yes, even a rule-breaker like Madonna.

You see, there is vast difference between what Simon the Pharisee stood for and what Jesus stood for. Simon was into throwing the rule book at people. Jesus was not. Simon loved pointing the finger. Jesus did not. Sadly, Christianity has occasionally had a reputation as a religion of guilt and 'pointing the finger'. Even sadder is the fact that many people who claim to follow Jesus have acted just like that. They seem to thrive on condemning people for their bad lifestyle. But this is not the religion of Jesus. It may have been Simon's favourite pastime, but Jesus took a very different approach.

AN UNANSWERED QUESTION

A more recent artist, pop singer Alanis Morissette, has an excellent song on one of her albums called *Forgiven*. In it she talks quite honestly about her experience as a teenager at a religious high school. The version of religion she was fed pointed the finger and made her feel guilty. In her own words, she and her friends had "no fun with no guilt-feelings". As a result, Alanis flaunted those rules—"What I learned I rejected". If the lyrics on the rest of the album are anything to go by, it seems Morissette has wandered a long way from the religion she was brought up with, and broken a lot of rules along the way.

Alanis Morissette is like many people who have been put off religion because of its apparent coldness. She, like many others, made a decision to keep religion at arm's length and refuse to follow its guilt-based moral standards. But there's a twist in her song, and I suspect it's a twist quite a few of us go through in life. In the final verse the whole tone of the song changes. Alanis appears more thoughtful, even regretful about her past. In her own words, the song is something of an "inquisition"—something that forces her to look at her life in a fresh way. She sings, "What I learned I rejected, but I believe again". It's as if the years since her high school days have made her rethink her previous thoughts about religion. But that raises a very uncomfortable question, or what she calls, "One last stupid question". It's a question that bugs her; a question she'd love an answer to. And so in the last line of the final verse she yells it out, "Will I be forgiven?"

That's a good question. In the previous chapter, we saw that Jesus possesses God's *authority* to forgive. But that doesn't answer the question, "Does he have the *inclination* to forgive me?" I mean it's one thing to forgive the wrongs of a reasonably innocent-looking cripple, but it's another thing to forgive someone who is a serious rule-breaker; someone who has wandered a long way from religion and its rules. Is it possible for someone who has totally rejected or ignored God to come back and find forgiveness? Sadly, there is nothing in Alanis Morissette's music, before or since, that suggests she knows the answer to her own question. For her, it is an unanswered question. Even sadder, there's nothing to suggest Madonna is even asking the question.

But Morissette's unanswered question does not have to remain unanswered for us. If Jesus' treatment of this 'sinful woman' is any clue, the answer has to be a very loud, "Yes!" If Jesus can look a rule-breaker like her in the eye and, in front of a group of religious bigots, say "Your sins are forgiven", he can do it for you and me too. No matter what we have done in the past, Jesus is *able* and *willing* to forgive us. What a relief it would be to know that despite our inconsistencies and failures God accepts us! How refreshing it would be if the baggage of our past was removed, and the stains of our lives wiped clean. This episode in Jesus' life is like an invitation to us from God to enjoy just that.

CHAPTER

9

TO BE TERMINATED

JESUS' CV IS LOOKING impressive. One day he's calming a storm; the next he's bringing back the dead. One day he's sending demons running; the next he's outwitting religious experts. Jesus' followers must have been wondering by this stage: "Who is this?!" If you had seen all that they had, I am sure you'd be more than curious to know as well. According to the biographies, however, the apostles were too afraid to ask Jesus directly. They just kept on trying to work it out for themselves.

NOT YOUR AVERAGE SURNAME

Then, one day, the guessing ended. Jesus turned to his friends, and put them on the spot, asking them who they thought he was. It was a big day for Jesus' followers, in more ways than one. All the biographies mention this day, but I'll stay with Mark's account for now:

As they were walking along, he asked them, "What do people say about me?" The disciples answered, "Some say you are John the Baptist or maybe Elijah. Others say you are one of the prophets".

Then Jesus asked them, "But who do you say I am?"

I think this is a question you'd want to have a good think about before you answered. Imagine spending a year or so with a man who not only does things like walk through hospitals and heal everyone, but also hands out God's forgiveness to whoever wants it, and then one day having him turn to you out of the blue and ask, "Who do you think I am?"

It's an answer you'd want to get right.

Peter, one of Jesus' closest friends, had been giving this a lot of thought. He'd been with Jesus ever since the beginning of his public career. He had seen it all. Here's what he said:

Peter answered, "You are the Christ".

I used to think 'Christ' was Jesus' surname. That meant Joseph and Mary would have been Mr and Mrs Christ. I had no idea that there was no such thing as a surname in those days. The word 'Christ' is nothing like a surname. It was actually a title, like our 'Prime Minister' or 'Colonel'. The difference was that, for Jews, there was only one Christ. This title was reserved for the most awesome person imaginable. According to the Jewish Scriptures (the Old Testament), the Christ (which is also the same word for 'messiah' in a different language) was none other than God's personal ambassador—the man who bears all the authority of the Creator himself. It puts a new spin on our understanding of the name, Jesus CHRIST, doesn't it?

THE KING OF TWIST

But there is a twist! This must have been the most confusing day of Peter's life. As soon as Peter said, "You are the Christ", Jesus did a very strange thing. He told his friends to tell no one who he was. Can you imagine how confusing that must have seemed to them all? Who puts out a number one single and refuses to do any touring? Who becomes a top super-model then refuses any more publicity photos? Who on earth would accept the title 'Christ' and then insist that no one else knows about it?

But it gets worse. Jesus no sooner admits he is God's personal ambassador, than he tells his friends that everything is about to go horribly wrong.

Jesus began telling his disciples what would happen to him. He said, "The nation's leaders, the chief priests, and teachers of the Law of Moses will make the Son of Man suffer terribly. He'll be rejected and killed, but three days later he'll rise to life".

This is the opposite of what the disciples could have expected. The "nation's leaders" and the "chief priests" were the very people who would have been expected to crown the Messiah (Christ) as King. But according to Jesus, they were going to kill him instead. This would have been very hard to comprehend. If Jesus can powerfully control the environment, how on earth could a few puny politicians, priests and professors get the better of him? Why would someone with so much power allow himself to be "rejected and killed"? Let me try and explain the answer.

TERMINATED

You may have seen the Arnold Schwarzenegger *Terminator* films. They are classic Arnie—9/10ths shoot 'em up action, 1/10th script. In the sequel, *Terminator II: Judgement Day*, Schwarzenegger plays a humanoid robot sent back in time to protect John Connor, a young lad who is destined to grow up and save the world from global destruction. The problem is, there is another Terminator robot whose mission is to kill the boy and his mum. Throughout the film, Schwarzenegger displays incredible power, speed and accuracy, with a little panache thrown in—everything you could hope for in an action hero, except acting ability perhaps!

The final scene of the film is a battle between the two Terminators which takes place in a huge metal factory. After some amazing special effects, complete with Dolby surround sound, Schwarzenegger emerges triumphant. The bad Terminator was 'sent' into a molten pit. Everything looks complete. Sarah Connor, John Connor's mother, looks from the scaffolding over the pit and sighs, "It's over!"

"No!", replies Arnie, "There's one more chip." Sure enough, the technology that would one day lead to world destruction was a computer chip sitting in his head. If that chip fell into the wrong hands it would mean disaster. Schwarzenegger insists that he must be destroyed. It is the only way devastation can be avoided. He grabs hold of a chain attached to a large crane and orders Mrs Connor to lower him into the molten pit. With music booming, the final scene of the film pictures Arnie descending into the pit, giving his life away for the sake of the world.

Putting aside the fact that *Terminator II* is a shallow, action-fantasy film, there is something quite spectacular about the idea of an incredibly powerful man choosing to die for the sake of others, especially if the idea is a true story.

Jesus' life is no fantasy film. It is flesh and blood history, and no historian doubts it. It is a certifiable fact of history that a man known as Jesus Christ was executed by crucifixion on the outskirts of ancient Jerusalem around 33AD. But what was the meaning of his death? If the biographies of Jesus' life are allowed to speak, the answer is simple: Jesus was an incredibly powerful man who chose to die so that other people could be saved. The biographies of his life all agree on this point. They say that although Jesus could out-teach academics, drive out evil spirits, and control the environment, his central mission was not one of *conquering* but of *serving*. According to his own words, there would come a day, about a year and a half later, when "the nation's leaders, the chief priests, and teachers of the Law of Moses will make the Son of Man suffer terribly".

Jesus' life goal, as the 'Christ', was to give his life away for our benefit.

The rest of this book tries to come to grips with what his death means.

A HELL OF A WAY TO GO

"In two days of brutality
they did away with
thirty years of brilliance."

CHAPTER

10

GOD IN OUR SHOES

A MAN, WITH SLICKED back hair, designer suit and polished finger nails, appears on American television with a message for his large and faithful audience, and for me. "God", he insists, "wants our houses and cars to be luxurious, our lives pain-free, and our pantries forever full". To him, God is not harsh and vengeful. He is a God of prosperity, and this slick TV evangelist has the houses, cars and pantry to prove it.

A woman, half-drunk and oblivious to those around her, yells out across the crowded pub: "How can you say God loves us when he takes our loved ones?" She is speaking to me, a religious bloke. She demands that I explain how a God who is meant to love people could have allowed her closest family members to be killed in a train/car collision just weeks before our chance meeting. To her, God is a monster; a harsh and vengeful being. Her shattered life proves it.

Here are two very, very different pictures of what God is like. Both views are firmly believed and passionately expressed. Each comes with a personal life experience as proof. But which is right?

This raises a huge and seemingly unanswerable question: how on earth can we know what God is really like? These two examples show that using your personal experience to see what God is like will give you mixed messages—even contradictory ones. We are left with the very dark possibility that maybe there is no way of knowing what God is like after all. Maybe God is totally invisible to us.

A SLOB LIKE ONE OF US

Pop singer Joan Osborne 'came and went' back in June 96, when she had the No. 1 single for four weeks in a row. The song was titled 'One Of Us' and, apart from having a very cool guitar riff, it asked some very profound questions:

If God had a name, what would it be?

If God had a face, what would it look like?

In other words, what is God like? The song's own vague answer was, "Yeah, yeah, God is great. Yeah, yeah, God is good". Not the deepest comment I've ever heard, but the 'what if?' question in the chorus was brilliant. It asked, "What if God was one of us/Just a slob like one of us?" Some religious people got terribly upset with Osborne. They said it was 'blasphemy' to talk about God being a "slob". But I think it was an excellent question (especially the word "slob"). All it was doing was saying, "Wouldn't it be great if God became flesh and blood for a while, so we

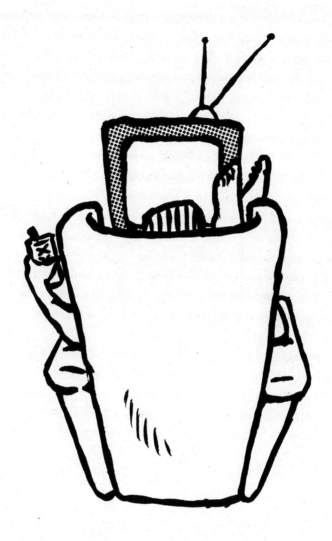

could see what he was like and ask all our questions!"

There is so much confusion and debate in our society about religion. Hindus insist there are many different gods (Shiva, Vishnu, etc.), but Jews demand there is only one. Buddhists say we are reincarnated after death, but Muslims say we are not. Who is right? Certainly not all of them. Perhaps none of them!

This is why I think Joan Osborne's song is so meaningful. Surely, the only way we can know for certain what God is like is if the *Creator* becomes part of the *creation* for a while—becomes one of us, just a slob like one of us! If God walked in our shoes for a while, we could see what sort of birth he'd choose. Would it be a traditional hospital or a trendy home birth? Would he go to a private school or public one? Would he vote Liberal, Labor, or Green? Would he listen to Radio National or Triple J? Would he frequent pubs or churches? More importantly, how would he treat people? What would he say to rock stars, or inmates in prison, or just the average person on the street like you and me? And if he ever had to die, like the rest of us, how would he cope with it?

STARING GOD IN THE FACE

For most of this book I've talked about Jesus as "God's ambassador". That is basically what the title 'Christ' means. But there was a day in his life when Jesus went way beyond this idea. It was a bizarre day! A day that staggered everyone who heard him.

It's Thursday night about 8pm. Jesus has just finished a meal with his close friends. This is not an ordinary Thursday however. It is the evening before Jesus' execution, except no one but Jesus (and the officials who were plotting his arrest) knows it. Jesus has been talking to his friends about "going away" and they are not happy with the idea. Who would be? Imagine being close friends with a man who can heal the sick, calm storms, raise the dead and forgive people's wrongs. I suspect you, like me, would want things to remain much the same.

The disciples start asking questions: "Where are you going? Why can't we come? How do we get to where you're going?" Then one of Jesus' friends, Philip, must have sensed that this was going to be the end of the fun and games. He starts to get very serious. This was his last chance to ask the one big question: a question not too different from the ones in Joan Osborne's old song. John's biography records it for us:

Philip said, "Lord, show us the Father. That's all we need".

Philip wants to know what every religion has always wanted to know: what is God (the "Father") like? Jesus' response was incredible.

Jesus replied, "Philip, I have been with you for a long time. Don't you know who I am? If you have seen me, you have seen the Father. How can you ask me to show you the Father? Don't you believe that I am one with the Father and the Father is one with me?"

Many of us think of Jesus as a truly 'good bloke' or as one of history's 'great teachers'. Both descriptions are no doubt true. But neither comes anywhere near this statement from Jesus' own lips. Jesus claimed not only to be God's ambassador, but God himself. He claimed to be God in our shoes; God as "one of us, just a slob like one of us".

If this makes you feel uncomfortable, spare a thought for poor old Philip. As a faithful Jew, Philip believed there is one God who created and controls the entire universe, and yet here was a man saying that looking at him is the same as looking at the very face of the Creator.

This must have been a very difficult concept for Philip and the others to comprehend, but it certainly would have explained a lot of their bizarre experiences over the last few years. The reason Jesus could out-teach all the academics of his day was because he knew everything. The reason he could overrule evil spirits was because he was the ultimate Spirit. The reason he could control the environment was because he created it. The reason he could raise a dead person to life was because he was the source of all life. The reason he could hand out God's forgiveness was because he in fact *was* God. Years before Joan Osborne asked, "What if God was one of us?", Jesus had given an answer!

THE BLASPHEMY OF CHRISTIANITY

I recently spoke on this topic at a university in Sydney. After I had finished my speech and sat down, a man in the audience began to publicly disagree with me. He stole the audience's attention and declared, "It is impossible! God would never become a human being. God is too big, too powerful. He would never limit himself to flesh and blood. It is absurd to think of God needing to eat, sleep or go to the toilet. What you have said is blasphemy!" The man was a devout and articulate Muslim. For the next 15 minutes or so, we entered into a public debate over the issue. In the end, I think it was a very important occasion for everyone in the lecture theatre. No one could have left the room thinking, "Oh, all the major religions teach basically the same thing". Just the opposite is the case. What is a "blasphemy" to Muslims, was, in fact, the crowning jewel of Jesus' teaching—God has become like one of us!

According to Islam, the God who demands our 'submission' (which is what the word 'Islam' means) is too powerful and awesome to live among us. But Jesus taught differently. He insisted that the God who demands our submission also shared our existence. He entered our 'flesh and blood' world to serve and save us, even if it meant getting his hands dirty—and bloody—in the process.

This has important implications for us. If Jesus is who he claimed to be, it means that we do not have to settle for the contradictory images of God we get from our own experience, or from endless religious debate. We *can* see what the Creator is like. We can know what kind of birth he'd choose, what sort of people he would mix with, and what things he would say. Put another way, Jesus' life is the picture that tells a thousand words about God.

This picture is carefully sketched in the pages of Jesus' biographies. There we are able to see him socialising at parties and teaching in religious settings. We are invited to hear his words of comfort at a funeral and his disturbing silence at his own public trial. We see him alone with friends and thundering in public debate. We observe him spending time with children and conversing with army generals and politicians. And, as we are about to see, these biographies allow us to witness Jesus being betrayed by a close friend, tried unjustly and then brutally tortured and executed. Reading these biographies is like being treated to front row seats in the most amazing show of all—God, walking in our shoes.

CHAPTER

11

JESUS' 'FATAL FLAW'

I ONLY REMEMBER a couple of things from my English classes at school. I recall that a *verb* is a 'doing word'. And for some bizarre reason I remember the little phrase, 'the fatal flaw' (it's no wonder I didn't do so well). Now this 'fatal flaw' (other people call it the 'tragic flaw') was interesting. My English teacher told us that in lots of plays, books and movies, the main character often had some personality trait that in the end got them killed. It was a 'flaw' (or defect) in their character that was tragic and fatal. Don't ask me why I remember this. Perhaps it was because I knew I had many flaws in my personality and wondered which one would prove 'fatal'.

Anyway, the more I thought about it, the more my teacher was right. Think of *Hamlet,* the Mel Gibson movie (apparently, this was a Shakespeare play first!). The main character in the story, Hamlet, procrastinates. He wants to take revenge for his father's death but he keeps putting it off. In the end, his procrastination is his downfall. It was his fatal flaw. Many classic Westerns also feature the fatal flaw. Often one of the main characters is so bold and arrogant he gets a reputation around town as a gunslinger. In the end though, it gets him shot. Then there's Superman. The fact that he comes from the planet Krypton makes him 'super', but even the man of steel crumbles around a piece of kryptonite. His fatal flaw is a bad allergy to homegrown rocks.

It may sound strange, but I think you could almost say that Jesus had a fatal flaw, too. There was something even in his personality that drove him toward danger. It was an unstoppable obsession. No matter who or what got in his way, Jesus had a mission, and it ended up getting him killed. If we can understand Jesus' fatal flaw, we'll understand the very heart of his career. That's what this chapter is all about.

FLOORED!

The one obvious thing about Jesus' life so far is that he's always been the man in control. He had control over storms; he was in command of the evil forces on the planet; he could walk into a funeral and ruin it by raising the dead person to life; he could out-debate all the best professors and politicians of his time. He was Mr Control!

But then comes Thursday night–his final night–and everything changes. Mr Control seems out of control. It's about 9 o'clock in the evening, and after having dinner with his closest friends, Jesus goes with them for a stroll in a nearby park, called the Garden of Gethsemane (which is still there today). After a while Jesus begins to act strangely:

> **Jesus took along Peter and the two brothers, James and John. He was very sad and troubled, and he said to them, "I'm so sad that I feel as if I'm dying. Stay here and keep awake with me". Jesus walked on a little way. Then he knelt with his face to the ground and prayed...**

Here is the man who was fazed by nothing all his life, now floored with sorrow. He is so upset he even asks his followers to stay awake with him. Whatever it is he's worried about, he doesn't want to do it alone. I don't know about you, but I'm a little uncomfortable with this. Imagine the strongest man in the world asking you to help him lift something, or the tallest man in the world asking you to help him reach something. Imagine Claudia Schiffer asking you for your beauty tips, or Michael Jordan asking you to help him shoot a basket from inside the free-throw area. You'd feel awkward, wouldn't you? Well, imagine what it was like for Peter, James and John. They had seen Jesus stop a thunder storm and now they were being asked to stay up and keep him company during his terrible sadness. The man they had seen stand up to anyone was now lying face down in the dirt, praying his heart out.

GOD IS NOT HAPPY!

So, what on earth made Jesus act like this? Here are Jesus' own words. These are the words he cried out to God as he lay on the ground. They tell us exactly what floored him.

> **... he knelt with his face to the ground and prayed, "My Father, if it's possible, don't make me suffer by having me drink from this cup. But do what you want, and not what I want".**

Jesus is afraid of a "cup". He's worried about drinking from a cup. When I first read this I didn't know what to make of it. Why would such a powerful man be terrified of drinking from a little cup? Then someone pointed out to me what the "cup" was all about. In the ancient world one of the best ways to assassinate someone (a king or some other official) was to spike their wine cup—a bit of poison in the cup and they've gone to meet their maker. (This is what happened in *Hamlet*, too.) From this, the term 'the cup' came to represent suffering or disaster. In the Old Testament (the first part of the Bible which Jesus often quoted), 'the cup' became a symbol of the disaster God would bring on individuals and whole countries who did evil things. In other words, the cup was a way of talking about God's punishment.

The cup image is a great reminder that God *does* see all the evil that goes on in the world. If you've watched videos like *Schindler's List, Mississippi Burning* or *In The Name of the Father,* like me you probably felt angry at the injustice and evil we humans have done to each other through the years. You may even have thought to yourself, "Why doesn't God do something about it?" Well, God feels that anger too—not because he's seen the films, but because, being God, he was there when these things took place. And, yes, he will do something about it. One day he'll pour out the 'cup' of his anger on everyone who deserves it.

The problem for us is that God doesn't only see international blockbuster evil—Nazi executions, racism, and false imprisonment. He sees the evil closer to home as well, and he's not happy. He sees what goes on in our schools, our workplaces, our homes. He even sees what goes on in our personal lives—everything we've done, said and thought. That anger we feel at the evil 'out there' could just as easily be directed at our own lives. Sure, you've most likely never mass-murdered Jews or hung black Americans. Nor have I. But the same selfishness and pride that led to these big things happening dwells in our hearts too. You only have to look at the bitching, back-stabbing and violence that happens in our schools, workplaces and homes to see that. God will do something about this 'evil', too. He will punish. Justice has to be done. That's what the image of the cup is all about.

PASS THE CUP

But the big question is: why on earth is Jesus face down in the dirt, terrified of drinking the cup of God's anger? Surely if anyone deserves to escape God's punishment, it's Jesus. Being perfect, he was in God's good books. The answer is simple: he isn't about to be punished for his own wrongs but for mine, and yours. Look at Jesus' words later that night as he continued to pray:

"My Father, if it is not possible for this cup to pass unless I drink it, may your will be done."

There is the answer—*it is not possible for the cup of God's anger to pass from you and me unless Jesus takes it for us*. In other words, Jesus is willing to recieve our punishment so that we don't have to.

Years ago, a young aboriginal man raped a girl from a neighbouring tribe. He then took off and was never seen again. The feeling between the two tribes was not good. Eventually, the elders met to work out how justice could still be done even though the rapist had run off. They decided that a man from the rapist's tribe should be chosen and punished for the crime of his fellow tribesman. The punishment was either a spear thrust into the man's thigh, or into the thigh and out the other side. They chose the second option. The 'lucky' man was presented before the elders and in went the spear (and out!). For these aborigines, justice was done. Now the two tribes could get on with each other again.

As gory as this story may sound to us, it does illustrate what Jesus meant by drinking the cup for us. Even though he had not wronged God in any way, he was willing to step forward and take the punishment we deserve.

So what was Jesus' 'fatal flaw'? What aspect of his personality would end up getting him killed? It was his unstoppable obsession to rescue people like you and me from getting what we deserve. He was so passionate about rescuing us from punishment that he was willing to die for it. Of course, this is not really a 'flaw' at all. In fact, for me, it's what makes Jesus stand out from the crowd of great leaders throughout the centuries. Here is a ruler who would rather die than see any of his followers recieve the punishment they actually deserve.

Just before midnight, a mob of angry officials and soldiers arrived at the Garden of Gethsemane to arrest Jesus. Jesus woke up his friends (according to Matthew's biography, they had fallen asleep under the stars while Jesus was baring his soul in prayer), and passively went with the soldiers.

What Jesus had told his friends a year and a half before, was about to take place. The Christ did not come to conquer but to suffer and die. That was his destiny. That was his 'cup' and it was about to be poured out.

CHAPTER

12

THE TRIAL OF YOUR LIFE

ON OCTOBER 5TH, 1974, the people of Guildford were down at their local pub enjoying a few quiet beers. With no warning at all a huge blast went off. It was a massive bomb—two bombs, actually. The pub was blown apart. Five people were killed and over sixty were severely injured. It was one of many terrorist bombings throughout England that year, but this one was going to be different. For this one, they were going to catch the murderers.

A few months later, Gerry Conlon was asleep in his family home in Ireland. Suddenly, soldiers armed with high-powered weapons burst into his bedroom. They dragged him out of bed, threw him into an army vehicle, drove him to an air base, and flew him straight to London. Before he knew it, Gerry found himself in a high security interrogation room being beaten by police. They kept him there for several days, not letting him eat, drink or sleep. After constant verbal and physical torture Gerry finally confessed to the Guildford bombing. The police had got what they wanted. They had caught their terrorist. In a matter of weeks Gerry was tried and convicted of the bombing and was sent to prison. He got thirty years.

There was a problem though. Gerry Conlon had nothing at all to do with the bombing. He was completely innocent. The only evidence against him was his confession which he had only given because he could no longer take the beatings, the sleep deprivation and the starvation.

Gerry's father was also sent to prison for the bombing, and died while in there. He also had nothing to do with the crime. He, too, was completely innocent.

In 1989, after serving 15 years for a crime he didn't commit and losing his father, Gerry was let out of prison. The police and courts admitted to the world they had made a 'mistake'.

The details are different of course, but what happened to Gerry Conlon has an awful lot in common with what happened to Jesus. Jesus, too, was arrested by armed soldiers, interrogated, tortured, sent to trial and found guilty. Jesus, however, got more than 15 years.

It was Thursday night, some time before midnight, and Jesus was arrested by the soldiers and taken to Jerusalem city for an immediate trial. The religious and political leaders wanted Jesus dead and the best way to pull this off was to act fast and at night. That way no one could come to his defence. They had a problem though. Only the Roman Governor could hand out the death penalty. So, after conducting their own trial and torture, the Jewish leaders took their prisoner straight to the most powerful man in the country, a brutal and successful military commander named Pontius Pilate.

JESUS VS THE EMPIRE

About 6am Friday morning, after hours of interrogation and beatings, Jesus was presented to Pilate. I'm sure Pilate had no idea his verdict that day would change the course of history. Jesus' biographies give us a brief summary of what went on in this early morning court case. Just like Gerry Conlon's case, Jesus' trial was a weird combination of lies, hatred and brutality.

According to each of the biographies, the trial of Jesus centred on one very serious crime–claiming to be a king. Here's part of the trial, taken straight out of Mark's biography:

Early the next morning the chief priests, the nation's leaders, and the teachers of the Law of Moses met together with the whole Jewish council. They tied Jesus up and led him off to Pilate.

He asked Jesus, "Are you the king of the Jews?"

"Those are your words", Jesus answered.

The question Pilate asked was a tricky one. The answer is 'yes' and 'no'. Jesus never claimed to be a 'king' in a political sense, so he wasn't a threat to the Roman empire as he was accused of being. He did, however, claim to have another kind of authority–God's authority to heal, calm storms, raise the dead, forgive wrongs and teach people how to live. In this sense I guess he was a king. In fact, he was the most powerful leader ever.

This is very important to understand. Many of us have been brought up to think of Jesus as a nice and gentle religious man. The Jesus films make him out to be like Ghandi; the Christmas cards portray him as a helpless baby lying in a manger; and some of our modern church statues present him as a skinny, naked man dying on a cross. Now, of course, it is true that Jesus was once a baby and it's true he was stripped naked and nailed to a cross. But Jesus was never viewed as a harmless religious guru. As we have already seen, those who met him were often in awe of him. His friends worshipped him as God. His enemies feared him as a threat. But no one ever thought he was a wimp. It was an eyeopening moment for me when I discovered that what led to Jesus' arrest and trial was the fact that thousands and thousands of people believed that he was God's appointed ruler of humanity.

THE TWISTED VERDICT

When Pilate asked Jesus about whether or not he was a leader, Jesus did not deny it. From that moment on, his fate was virtually sealed. The Roman empire would stand for no other leader, even if he wasn't strictly a political leader.

By this time, the crowds outside the court were screaming for Jesus' death. It must have looked like our modern scene where crowds wait outside the court when a multiple rapist is being tried. Although Pilate was a brutal military leader, he (like many leaders) was also a crowd-pleaser. He knew Jesus posed no political threat, but he thought it would cause less problems to agree with the cries for blood he could hear outside the palace. And so Jesus was found guilty of treason against the Roman empire and sentenced to death by crucifixion. In so doing, Pilate made the worst error of judgement in his career.

What happens then is awful. Before executing Jesus, Pilate has him tortured. The soldiers take the opportunity to turn it into a sick game. Here's how Mark's biography describes it:

Pilate...ordered his soldiers to beat Jesus with a whip and nail him to a cross.

The soldiers led Jesus inside the courtyard of the fortress and called together the rest of the troops. They put a purple robe on him, and on his head they placed a crown that they had made out of thorny branches. They made fun of Jesus and shouted, "Hey, you king of the Jews!" Then they beat him on the head with a stick. They spat on him and knelt down and pretended to worship him.

The whips used in these ancient floggings had pieces of lead and bones imbedded into a leather strap. It was designed to rip the flesh off a victim's back, and weaken them for the execution. The thorns of the date palm in that part of the world grow up to 20cm long. Twisted together and stuck on someone's head, they would have made a dramatic (and cruel) looking crown. So picture this: Jesus has already suffered the betrayal of a friend, a sleepless night, hours of questioning, a couple of beatings and a flogging. Then a whole company of soldiers (it could have been at least 50 men) start to spit on him and beat him with wooden poles (like a modern police baton). To top it off, they make a sick joke of bowing down before him and saying, "Hey, you king of the Jews". Even if Jesus wasn't a king, this is still cruel. But what if he was?

THE VERDICT TWISTED

Just as Gerry Conlon was eventually proved right, so Jesus was proved right. When Jesus was raised from the dead a few days after his execution (a topic we'll look at later), it was the ultimate proof that Jesus was who he said he was—God's powerful leader of the world. That meant that everyone who rejected Jesus was very wrong!

This has terrible implications. When Gerry Conlon was proved right it exposed the British police as guilty of a terrible evil. A friend of mine was in England when Conlon was released from prison. He says the feeling throughout England was one of incredible shame. Not only were the police guilty, but everyone who wrongly condemned Gerry Conlon (the judge, the jury, the media and the average person on the street) was guilty of a terrible mistake. In falsely condemning Gerry, they were actually condemning themselves. Let me make this clearer.

Imagine I go to see the London Philharmonic Orchestra. After the concert I criticise them as a bunch of boring, untalented musicians. That would tell you far more about *my* musical ability than the skill of the orchestra, wouldn't it? Or suppose I go to the art gallery to see some paintings by Monet. During the exhibition I judge the paintings as dull and simplistic, the sort of thing a kid could paint. That tells you far more about my artistic ability than Monet's, doesn't it? When I *falsely* judge something (like the London Philharmonic Orchestra or Monet's paintings) it is actually a judgement of me. If this is true of small things like music and art, how much more is it true of huge things like condemning Gerry Conlon to life imprisonment? By wrongly condemning Gerry, the police were condemning themselves.

It's the same with Jesus, only much bigger. The people who condemned Jesus were actually condemning themselves. In making a wrong judgement about Jesus they were bringing judgement on themselves. The Jewish leaders plotted against Jesus and falsely accused him. Pontius Pilate handed down the death sentence. And the soldiers beat and mocked him. Everyone that day rejected Jesus as King. But everyone that day was wrong. As far as God was concerned, it was them who were on trial, not Jesus. Their verdict about Jesus would end up being God's verdict about them.

So, what has this got to do with us? We weren't there that day, so there's no way we could be blamed for condemning Jesus, is there? Of course not! But there is a question we must ask ourselves. What is *our* verdict about Jesus *today*? Sure, we weren't there the day Jesus was condemned, but he isn't back there anymore either. He has literally been raised from the dead. He is alive right now! If Jesus ever *was* God's appointed leader over the world, he still *is* today. That has implications for me, right here and now. I need to work out whether I now accept him as my leader (king) or, like Pilate, the soldiers and the Jewish leaders, reject him as a fraud.

Our verdict about Jesus will determine God's verdict about us. So as you think about all that happened to Jesus at his trial, remember, it is also your trial (and mine). What you decide about Jesus is actually the trial of *your* life.

CHAPTER

13

A HELL OF A LIFE

DURING THE PEAK OF his career as the Heavyweight Boxing Champion of the world, Muhammad Ali was flying interstate across America for one of his title fights. Suddenly, the captain announced, "Ladies and gentlemen, will you please fasten your seat belts? We are about to enter a storm and will experience some quite severe turbulence". For a captain to be that blunt about turbulence, it had to be bad. Immediately, everyone did as they were told. That is, everyone except Ali. He was sitting confidently up in First Class with his belt obviously undone.

When the flight attendant, who was checking everyone's seat belt, saw Muhammad she said, "Sir, the captain has asked us to fasten seat belts. We are about to enter a storm and it could be dangerous". He replied, "Superman don't need no seat belt". Quick as a flash, the flight attendant answered him, "Superman don't need no plane".

The arrogance, 10km above the ground, in a great big piece of aluminium (let's face it, that's all planes are), in the middle of a dangerous

storm, to say that you do not need a seat belt! The reality was, he needed the seat belt. In fact, he needed the flight attendant, and the Captain, and also the plane!

For some of us, the hardest thing to do in the world is admit our weakness and failure. Despite all good sense, we pretend we're Superwoman or Superman. This is particularly the case when it comes to religion. For some bizarre reason, some of us (I include myself) have at times thought, "I'm doing fine on my own. I don't need God". The more I think about it, the more this sounds like Muhammad Ali in the middle of that storm.

By about 10am Friday morning, three men found themselves in front of a large crowd, nailed hand and foot to huge wooden cross-like structures. They were naked, bleeding, dying. Each of them was being executed for very serious crimes—one of them, for the most serious crime. It was the end of the line for these guys. There were no more ambitions, no more parties, no more friendships and, in several hours, no more breathing! You would think that in a situation like this, all three men would be feeling quite *un*-super.

Amazingly, though, one of them refuses to face up to the reality of this situation. Not only is this man experiencing the shame and agony of being crucified in front of an audience, he is about to meet his Maker. He is in serious trouble. Instead of coming to his senses, though, he turns to the man being crucified in the middle, about five or ten metres away, and yells abuse at him. Luke's biography records this for us:

One of the criminals who hung there, hurled insults at Jesus, saying, "Aren't you the Christ. Save yourself and us!"

From about 5 or 6 in the morning, leaders, politicians, soldiers and Pontius Pilate, have all been abusing Jesus and making fun of his claim to be 'the Christ'. Now this dying criminal joins in. He joins a long line of people that day who made the terrible mistake of falsely judging Jesus. His words say it all. This man thinks he has no need of Jesus. Perhaps he thinks he is Superman.

TIME FOR A LITTLE HONESTY

The most amazing thing about this event is the reaction of the second criminal—the man crucified on the other side of Jesus. He had been doing some serious thinking about his situation. As soon as he hears these insulting words from the first criminal, he yells to him from fifteen or twenty metres away (from the other side of Jesus):

"Don't you fear God, since you are under the same penalty? We are punished justly, for we are getting what our deeds deserve. But this man has done nothing wrong!"

Over the years I have spoken with many inmates in prison. But I don't think I have ever heard one of them be as open about their crime and sentence as this man. Unlike the other criminal, he knows he is about to meet his Maker. He understands this is not the time for playing Superman. This is the time to fasten the seat belt, listen to the flight attendant, obey the captain, and pray that the aircraft makes it through the storm! In other words, this is the time for being honest about his weakness and failures.

Isn't it a relief to be honest about our lives? In the film *Dead Man Walking* (based on a true story), Sister Helen Prejean is the spiritual advisor to Matthew Poncelet, a convicted killer on death row. For the few days before his execution by lethal injection, Poncelet refuses to face up to his crime. He won't admit to himself, to Sister Helen, or to God that he has done wrong. The tension in the film is awful as Sister Helen begs him to own up to his actions. Finally, at 11:40pm on the 13th of March 1994, with 20 minutes to go before his death, Poncelet breaks down in tears and admits what he has done (to himself, Sister Helen and God). The sense of relief I felt watching this scene was amazing. I thought to myself, "What a relief it is to be honest about the state of our lives!" I don't just mean for criminals like Matthew Poncelet or the man crucified next to Jesus. I mean for people like you and me. Sure, we may not have committed criminal offences but God isn't only interested in those type of actions. The word Jesus often used—'sin'—has to do with falling short of God's standards, not our society's laws. Who of us can claim *not* to have broken *God's* standards? Who of us can claim *not* to have dark things in our lives for which we are ashamed? Not me! Someone once said, "Humans are the only species that can blush. And the only one that should". I agree.

A FINAL APPEAL TO THE KING

This criminal, however, does more than just feel bad about himself. He doesn't just admit his failures in front of everyone—the other criminal, the crowd, and Jesus—he does something about it:

And he said to Jesus, "Remember me when you come as King!"

Earlier that morning, the politicians and religious leaders had accused Jesus of treason for claiming to be God's King (or the Christ). The police had shoved a crown of thorns on his head, and punched him in the face, sarcastically yelling, "Hey, King!" Pontius Pilate then sealed Jesus' fate by finding him guilty of pretending to be King and handing down the death sentence. Everyone refused to acknowledge Jesus as the Christ or King. But the very thing everyone rejected, one person that day accepted. The criminal dying next to Jesus begs him, "Remember me when you come as KING!" Despite the fact that Jesus is also naked, bleeding and about to die, this criminal can see that Jesus is exactly who he claimed to be.

The criminal must have thought to himself, "If Jesus really is God's King, he has the ability to give me a place in God's kingdom". And so he asks, "Remember me!" I love these words because they are so unreligious and unpretentious. He doesn't say, "Oh Lord, Thou art holy and great, and I am but a worm. In Thy Mercy, forgivest mine iniquities". His words are simple and sincere. He is merely asking THE KING for a small place in THE KINGDOM.

COMING HOME

Jesus response is typical. It's brilliant!

Remember Jesus has got his own problems at this point. He also has nails as thick as your fingers through his hands and feet. He is also naked in front of a largely unsympathetic crowd. He also is about to die. But Jesus responds in true style:

Jesus said to him, "I promise you that today you will be in Paradise with me".

Instant, total, unconditional acceptance—that's what Jesus gave this criminal! No questions asked, no requirements set out, no 'ifs and buts', nothing! The man had admitted his failure; he had acknowledged Jesus as King; and he had asked the King personally for mercy. That's enough. That's what it means to respond to Jesus. That's how people can find his forgiveness. Those that day who played Superman or Superwoman would have soon found out how un-super they really were. But the man dying next to Jesus was about to find out that the best and safest way to travel through life is to fasten the seat belt and listen to the Captain.

I read a true story a while ago about a young girl in Brazil named Christina. She, like heaps of teenagers in the country, grew up with a passion to experience the exciting life of the capital, Rio, a city known for it's party life. Early one morning, before light, she ran away from home. She headed straight for the city. When her mum woke up later that morning and discovered Christina had gone, she was devastated. She knew exactly what her daughter was doing. She'd often heard her talking about going to the city. But Christina's mum knew that she would not find work in Rio. The only work a pretty young teenager would easily find in Rio was prostitution. Her mum headed straight to the city to begin her search.

After searching for some time, Christina's mum decided to make copies of photos of herself, write a little message on the back of them, and place them in all the sleazy bars and brothels she could find. After doing this, she went back home.

Sure enough, Christina had found no work. She did in fact turn to prostitution. The bright lights of Rio were not so attractive after all. But she couldn't go home—not after what she'd done. Sometime later, however, Christina was in one of those sleazy joints her mum had visited and, to her utter amazement, noticed a photo of her mum pinned to the wall. She grabbed it, then noticed the little message written on the back. She turned it over and read these words: "Whatever you have done, whatever you have become, please come home!" Apparently, that's exactly what she did.

What a beautiful story of human forgiveness this is! But more than that, what a beautiful picture of God's forgiveness! In a way, the more inspiring story of the forgiven criminal next to Jesus, is a little like a personal note from the ultimate parent to you and me saying, "Whatever you have done, whatever you have become, please come home!"

Within moments of hearing Jesus' words of acceptance, the forgiven criminal witnessed a very strange and awful event in human history. Luke's biography continues:

Around midday the sky turned dark and stayed that way until the middle of the afternoon. The sun stopped shining. Jesus shouted, "Father, I put

myself into your hands!" Then he died.

A crowd had gathered to see the terrible sight. Then after they had seen it, they felt broken-hearted and went home.

Imagine being in the crowd that day. You've listened to these three dying men shouting to each other—one abusing Jesus; one begging Jesus for mercy; and Jesus himself promising him a place in his kingdom. Then, some time after this conversation, a bizarre darkness covers the city—the sun looks like it has stopped shining. Then the man on the centre cross becomes more restless. He yells out and dies, and the blackout remains for three more hours. What would you have thought? I bet, at the very least, you would have thought, "Something quite awesome is happening". And you'd be dead right!

I often wonder how much the criminal dying next to Jesus understood of what Jesus was doing. I wonder if he realised that he could be forgiven only because Jesus was being punished. I wonder if he knew that forgiveness was free for him only because it was costly for Jesus; that he received mercy only because Jesus drank the cup of God's judgement; that he was given a clean slate in life only because Jesus took on his guilty record. The criminal was about to enjoy Paradise, but only because Jesus experienced Hell.

This book is called *A Hell Of A Life* for two reasons. First, because Jesus' life was so incredible. It was a life full of action, danger, mystery and power. But there is a more unusual and serious reason for the title. According to Jesus himself, the focus of his whole life's work was to die for you and me. He did this so that we (not just criminals) could be forgiven by God, instead of punished by him. Put simply, he took Hell for us, so that we wouldn't have to. Jesus had 'a hell of a life', so that we (like the man dying next to Jesus) could 'come home' to God.

A SERIOUS COMEBACK

"Over a billion people now think he runs the world. Either it's the biggest scam in history, or he pulled off one serious comeback."

WARNING!

If only the biographies of Jesus' life had ended their story with the death of Jesus! That would still have left us with one of the most moving stories of history—a tough, loving, heroic man betrayed and killed by proud, power-hungry politicians. It's the sort of stuff great movies are made of. But no, they had to go and make the most outrageous claim of all time. They had to go and insist that a few days after his execution Jesus was back from the dead.

The claim about Jesus' resurrection does one of two things to the story of Jesus' life. If the claim is false, it robs the entire story of any credibility. It becomes just another myth or legend from the past. I mean, if the resurrection bit is phoney, how can we trust anything they told us? How can we be sure Jesus ever taught with incredible authority, or healed, or calmed a storm, or handed out God's forgiveness? On the other hand, if the claim is true, it elevates the story to dizzy heights. It makes Jesus the most unique and confronting person in human history.

It would be absurd to write a book about Jesus without staring the issue of his resurrection in the face; so we'll stare at it for two whole chapters. The first one ('For those who like a good argument'), will deal with the intellectual arguments for and against Jesus' resurrection. Let me warn you, it may be hard going if you don't like a good argument. The second chapter ('Alive and Kicking') is very different. There I'll try to explain what Jesus' resurrection means for us today. If you don't like arguments, I suggest you jump straight there. It's a far more important chapter anyhow.

CHAPTER

14

FOR THOSE WHO LIKE A GOOD ARGUMENT

SO, DID JESUS RISE FROM THE DEAD?

For centuries people have tried to rule out the whole discussion about 'resurrection' as ridiculous. They say, "Dead people just do not come back to life, so Jesus can't have been raised from the dead". That is, because we have never seen a resurrection we rule it out as a possibility. At first, this seems fair enough. I mean, I've never seen a pink and polka dot coloured elephant so I rule it out as a possibility.

However, there's a problem with this. The problem has to do with the rules of logic. Limited observation does not establish fixed laws. Or put simply, just because we've never seen something, doesn't mean it doesn't exist. For example, if you lived in England two centuries ago, you would have been brought up to believe that all swans were white. You would have dismissed the rumours about black swans (coming from Southern Hemisphere countries like Australia and South Africa) as wild hoaxes or a case of mistaken identity. But the fact of the matter is, black swans did exist even though the English had never seen them. You see, limited observation can only help you predict what to expect. It can't determine what actually is. So, according to the rules of logic, an 18th century Englishman could only say, "Having never seen a black swan in the past, I do not expect to see one in the future. Further evidence is required before I accept the existence of black swans".

The same is true of Jesus' resurrection. It can't be ruled out merely by logic. But it is fair enough to ask to see some evidence. This, of course, raises a few questions:

- Is there good evidence to support Jesus' resurrection?
- Is this evidence strong enough to contradict our expectation that resurrections don't happen?

I think there are four pieces of evidence that suggest Jesus was raised from the dead. I'll present each of them and then raise some arguments against them. You can be the judge of whether or not the evidence is strong.

1. JESUS' TOMB WAS CORPSE-LESS

One of the most compelling reasons *for* Jesus' resurrection is the fact that it is almost beyond doubt that Jesus' tomb was empty, a short time after his execution.

There are three things that make the empty tomb virtually beyond doubt.

A. JESUS' RESURRECTION WAS PROCLAIMED IN JERUSALEM JUST WEEKS AFTER THE CRUCIFIXION.

This is very important. If Jesus' tomb was not empty, such preaching could not have taken place. The tomb was owned by a prominent politician of the time named Joseph of Arimathea and so could easily be found by anyone who wanted to know. How on earth would the apostles have got away with telling people in Jerusalem (where Jesus was buried) that they had seen Jesus alive and well, without a body being produced to contradict them? Let me put it like this. Down at Balmoral Beach in Mosman, Sydney (near where I live) there is a statue of a dog named 'Billy'. He was a well-known canine in the area years ago. Suppose next week I claim to have seen the statue of Billy the wonder dog come to life and run away. Now, I might just get away with that claim in Perth or New Zealand (no offence meant), where no one could check up on me. But I couldn't get away with it in Mosman itself, could I? Mosman residents could too easily take a drive down to the beach and prove me a liar. The fact is, the first public claim of Jesus' resurrection occurred less than five kilometres from his burial site. This is a strong reason to be confident the tomb was, in fact, empty.

B. JESUS' TOMB DID NOT BECOME A HOLY SITE IN THE YEARS IMMEDIATE-LY AFTER HIS DEATH.

Now this doesn't sound very interesting on it's own, I know. But what is odd, is that during the time of Jesus there were at least 50 tombs of great religious leaders in Palestine, and all of these sites were considered to be holy sites. A fair bit of religious activity took place at them. So, the question needs to be asked, "If Jesus' corpse remained in the tomb, why was this custom not followed?"

C. THE JEWISH LEADERS DID NOT CONTEST THE EMPTY TOMB.

In Matthew's biography, it is clear that the popular argument against Jesus' resurrection in the years following the claim did not revolve around *whether* the tomb was empty but *how* it got empty. It was assumed, even by those who violently opposed the disciples' claim, that the tomb of Jesus was vacant and had been so from a couple of days after his execution. There's even an ancient document a hundred years after this that records a debate between a Jewish intellectual named Trypho and a Christian leader named Justin. In the document it is clear the Jews of that time still did not argue against the tomb being empty. They simply raised suspicion about how it got to be empty!

So the obvious question is, "How did the tomb get empty?" Here are a few explanations:

Perhaps Jesus didn't die on the cross, but simply fell unconscious, was buried, and later got better in the tomb.

According to this explanation, Jesus unwrapped his own burial clothes, rolled away the boulder that blocked the entrance, walked for two or three kilometres, showed himself to his friends and was somehow able to convince them that God had powerfully raised him to a new life. All I can say to this explanation is that it *used* to be argued. Modern scholars are now a bit embarrassed that this argument was ever used. The more we've learnt about Roman execution in the period, the more impossible it looks that Jesus just 'got better' in the tomb, let alone convinced his friends that he was powerfully alive and well.

Perhaps they went to the wrong tomb on Sunday morning.

Jesus' tomb was visited by some women who were his followers. They were the ones who discovered the tomb was empty. Some people think they visited the wrong tomb.

This explanation suggests that the tomb Mary and the other women went to *looked like* the one Jesus was placed in, but in actual fact was another one that happened to be unused. Thus, the whole of Christianity is based on a couple of people losing their way in the night. Apart from sounding stupid (at least to my ears) this explanation faces the very serious problem that sooner or later someone would have checked again. Remember, the tomb where Jesus was buried was owned by one of the prominent politicians of the time. It could have easily been accessed and the women's mistake would have been revealed.

Perhaps the disciples stole the body and later claimed he was raised.

This is the oldest explanation of the empty tomb (actually it's the second oldest!). It's the one Jewish people have used ever since the 1st century. For me, though, it is also the hardest to accept. Think of it this way. Suppose I stand up in church next week and claim to have seen the statue of 'Billy' the wonder dog come to life and run away. After a thorough search of Balmoral Beach, it is discovered that the statue is missing. Within weeks I'm a national celebrity. Triple J's radio host Jen Oldershaw invites me onto her show and praises me for having seen a modern miracle. Ray Martin rings me offering a million dollar contract for the exclusive rights to a step-by-step re-enactment of the miracle. Rupert Murdoch wants to publish my story and Oxford University offers me an honorary Doctorate in the Metaphysics of Animated Statues. What would you conclude? I'm sure some of you would be thinking, "I bet he stole the statue for his own personal gain". I reckon that's what I'd conclude too.

But suppose things went the other way. Jen Oldershaw grills me for being a scam artist (a very scary thought indeed!). Ray Martin exposes me as a fraud. My family disowns me. Rupert Murdoch prints an article about the stupidity of belief in animated statues. I am eventually taken to court and tried for 'public deception', and then taken to prison until I admit to the truth. If I *had* stolen the statue, how long do you think it would take before I confessed to my deception? Not long I think.

The same problem applies to Jesus' resurrection. If the disciples had become rich and famous for their claims about Jesus, it would be easier to conclude that they stole the body from the tomb and made up this incredible resurrection story. But the opposite is true. They were considered 'heretics' and 'traitors' by many of their fellow Jews. They were taken to court and thrown in prison. And many of them were, in fact, executed. Why, if they knew they had merely taken the body from the tomb, did they die for the claim that Jesus was raised from the tomb? Sure, plenty of people throughout history have suffered and died for beliefs they did not know were wrong, but who on earth would willingly die for something they knew was a lie? I just find it almost impossible to accept.

In my opinion, none of these attempts to explain away the empty tomb succeeds. This brings me back to my first piece of evidence. It seems almost beyond doubt that the tomb of Jesus was actually corpseless on Easter Sunday morning, and no attempt to explain it away satisfies the facts. In the words of historian, Paul L. Maier:

If all the evidence is weighted carefully and fairly, it is indeed justifiable, according to the canons of historical research, to conclude that the tomb in which Jesus was buried was actually empty on the morning of the First Easter.

Let me quickly offer a few more pieces of evidence for the resurrection of Jesus.

2. WOMEN WERE THE FIRST WITNESSES TO THE RESURRECTION
One of the interesting features of the biographies is that they all claim that women were the first people to witness the event. This may not sound like a very big deal to us modern onlookers, but in 1st century

Palestine it was a very significant point. A woman's testimony was considered untrustworthy by many 1st century Jewish leaders, so much so that they were not allowed to give evidence in a court of law. I know this sounds horrible but this was the legal situation of the time (incidentally, the fact that women *were* the first to witness the resurrection shows that God had no problem with this).

This being the case, the question must be asked, "If you had made up a lie about a man rising from the dead, why would you add that women were the first witnesses?" In Jewish society this would have only worsened their outrageous claim. Unless it was just plain TRUE, why would all four biographies agree that women were the first to witness Jesus' resurrection?

3. SIMILARITIES AND DISSIMILARITIES IN THE ACCOUNTS

A third reason *for* the resurrection of Jesus has to do with the nature of the biographies themselves. On the one hand, the different accounts agree in profound ways. For example, they agree on the day it occurred and that it was morning when it happened. They agree that women were the first to realise the resurrection had taken place. And they agree that there was confusion and doubt among the apostles when they first heard he was raised. However, someone could look at all this 'agreement' and argue that the biographers just got together and made sure they all said the same thing.

However, the hole in this argument is that there are also significant differences between the biographies. And some of these differences are very difficult (though not impossible) to reconcile with each other. For example, Mark's biography says that just after daylight on Sunday morning, three women first went to the tomb. John's biography, however, mentions only one woman, and she apparently visited while it was still dark.

My point is, if all the accounts were full of contradictions you could conclude they were not trustworthy. But if they were identical, word for word, you could conclude there was a planned scam or cover-up. But neither looks likely. The different biographies display both profound agreement and significant variation. This is exactly what you'd expect from four relatively independent people telling the truth about the same event.

Someone I know gave a copy of the four biographies of Jesus' life to a Sydney cop who was questioning the believability of Christianity. After reading the different accounts, he was impressed. In fact, he commented that when police investigate a crime they look for similarities and differences between the various witness reports. It's the blend of general agreement and partial difference between the reports that makes police confident they are reading a trustworthy account. This cop thought the biographies of Jesus' life, and in particular the accounts of the resurrection, looked like good witness reports.

4. TRANSFORMATION OF THE DISCIPLES

A fourth piece of evidence *for* the resurrection is the amazing transformation of Jesus' disciples after Easter Sunday. How did a small group of uneducated Jewish people become so adamant about their leader's resurrection that they confidently claimed, proclaimed, debated, stood trial, suffered and, in some cases, died, for that claim? And, how on earth did devout 1st century Jews (who naturally avoided other races and nations), begin the largest, most international and multicultural religion in the world?

Let me give you an individual example of the transformation that took place in one of Jesus' followers. In the biographies it is clear that Jesus' own brothers (yes, he had a few brothers) did not believe in him. In fact, according to Mark's biography, early on, they thought their famous brother was insane. However, in the Bible book called 'Acts', which describes the first years of the church after Jesus' resurrection, one of Jesus' brothers, James, has somehow become a key leader of the early church. How did this happen? What caused the transformation of James if it wasn't seeing his own brother risen from the dead?

More than that, James eventually died for his belief in his older brother. The question is simple: what stands between the unbelief of James recorded in the biographies and his willingness to be executed for believing in the risen Jesus? What caused such a transformation if it was not that he had seen his brother raised from death? This is only one example. Several, if not most, of the Apostles were eventually executed for their beliefs in the risen Jesus. What caused such fearless devotion?

Over the years, there have been a number of attempts to explain away this transformation. Here are a few of them.

A. PERHAPS THE DISCIPLES SIMPLY SAW A 'VISION'

Some people have suggested what the apostles saw was not the raised body of Jesus but some religious vision, like the kind spoken of in many religions. The basic problem with this explanation is that the Bible is full of 'visions' and is happy to name them as such. There is no question that the eyewitnesses (and biographers) of Jesus' resurrection knew the difference between a vision and a real event. However, nowhere do they speak of the resurrection as a vision. People who suggest the resurrection was simply a religious vision are left with a dilemma: why did people who were well acquainted with visions claim that the resurrection was a real physical event?

B. PERHAPS THE DISCIPLES HALLUCINATED

Another explanation of the disciples' transformation suggests that after their terrible weekend–seeing their master executed, not sleeping or eating–the disciples may well have experienced hallucinations of Jesus which they thought were real. The problem with this explanation is that, to sane people, even hallucinations are identifiable as such after the event. Secondly, you have the problem of explaining how over 500 people in many settings could have had the same hallucination over a forty day period.

This transformation of the disciples is so difficult to explain that a leading modern scholar, Dr Pinchas Lapide, has admitted that Jesus' resurrection must have happened. This is not so amazing by itself–heaps of modern scholars believe Jesus rose from the dead. What is amazing is that Lapide is a devout Jew who adamantly opposes the Christian belief that Jesus was God's ambassador, or the Christ. Anyway, here is what he concludes:

> How was it possible that his disciples, who by no means excelled in intelligence, eloquence, or strength of faith, were able to begin their victorious march of conversion...In a purely logical analysis, the resurrection of Jesus is "the lesser of two evils" for all those who seek a rational explanation of the worldwide consequences of that Easter faith. Thus according to my opinion, the resurrection belongs to the category of the truly real...A fact which indeed is withheld from objective science, photography, and a conceptual proof, but not from the believing scrutiny of history which more frequently leads to deeper insights.*

What can I say? Well said, Pinchas!

---

* The quote by Jewish scholar Pinchas Lapide is from his book *The Resurrection of Jesus: a Jewish perspective* (London: SPCK, 1984)

CHAPTER

15

ALIVE AND KICKING

I **HEARD A STORY** about a man who woke up one morning absolutely convinced that he had died in the night. At the breakfast table he ate nothing. He just sat there moping. At first his friends and family thought he was playing a joke, but as the days passed they realised he really did believe he was dead. His wife eventually took him to a renowned psychiatrist, hoping he would be able to cure her husband's strange condition. After hours of therapy there was no change. Then, in desperation, the psychiatrist tried one last idea.

He got out his medical text books, turned to the chapters on death, and showed his patient one simple fact of the medical world—dead people do not bleed. After very carefully reading the pages himself and weighing the evidence, the patient agreed, "OK, I agree. Dead people do not bleed!" Immediately, the psychiatrist pulled out a small pin and jabbed it into the patient's arm. Blood spurted out everywhere. In utter amazement the patient looked at his bleeding arm and declared, "Well, what do you know, dead people do bleed after all".

In some ways, the previous chapter was an attempt to change a few minds—to present some of the evidence that has given me confidence in Jesus' resurrection. But as this little story illustrates, some people would rather be dead than budge in their opinions. I suppose some readers will reject the evidence presented in the previous chapter, and as a result, refuse to change their minds about Jesus. I can live with that! What you do with the evidence is completely up to you. There will be others though, I hope, who, like me, may have gained a new confidence in the possibility of Jesus' resurrection. If that's you, this chapter is written with you particularly in mind. That's not to say sceptics aren't welcome. Of course, you are. It's just that at this point I want to try to explain what it means to respond to Jesus' resurrection. I want to look at how Jesus himself expected people to respond to him after his almighty 'come-back', and what that means for people like us 2000 years later.

WHO'S THE BOSS?

One of the very interesting things about the resurrection of Jesus (apart from the event itself) is the reaction of Thomas, one of Jesus' close friends. John's biography records it for us:

> The disciples were afraid of the Jewish leaders, and on the evening of the same Sunday they locked themselves in a room. Suddenly, Jesus appeared in the middle of the group. He greeted them and showed them his hands and his side. When the disciples saw the Lord, they became very happy.
>
> Although Thomas the Twin was one of the twelve disciples, he wasn't with the others when Jesus appeared to them. So they told him, "We have see the Lord!"
>
> But Thomas said, "First, I must see the nail scars in his hands and touch them with my finger. I must put my hand where the spear went into his side. I won't believe unless I do this!"

The first person ever to reject the idea that Jesus was raised from the dead was not a sceptical enemy, but a sceptical fan. Thomas was a man who had known Jesus intimately. He had eaten meals with him, listened to his teaching, watched him do miracles. Even after all this, he still refused to believe Jesus could be alive. Even when his closest friends insisted they had seen Jesus, he would not accept it. Thomas wanted to see Jesus and touch the crucifixion wounds, or he wasn't going to believe.

I'm not sure if he expected to get his proof, but within a week Thomas got the shock of his life. John's biography continues:

> A week later the disciples were together again. This time, Thomas was with them. Jesus came in while the doors were still locked and stood in the middle of the group. He greeted his disciples and said to Thomas, "Put your finger here and look at my hands! Put your hand into my side. Stop doubting and have faith!"
>
> Thomas replied, "You are my Lord and my God!"

How did Jesus expect people to respond to his resurrection? The answer is simple. They were to totally submit to him as "Lord" and "God".

It is just as simple for us too. We can't see Jesus like Thomas did, but we can certainly respond in the same way. Put simply, Jesus expects us to treat him as THE BOSS! We are to acknowledge him as our King, Leader, Coach, Master, Lord, God, etc., etc. Let me illustrate this idea.

A CHANGE OF NAME

About three hundred years before Jesus was born, the greatest king the world knew was a man named Alexander the Great. He ran all over the ancient world conquering whichever country he wanted. His armies were virtually unstoppable. The mere mention of Alexander and his armies was enough to send other kings into a fearful spin.

I heard a true story a while ago about a young soldier in Alexander's army who made a very unwise career move—he went AWOL. He abandoned his duties and fled from sight. The young man was soon found, however, and brought before a furious King Alexander. Can you imagine being that soldier? You've just betrayed the most powerful man in the known world, and now you're standing in his palace right in front of him. The penalty was usually instant execution for this kind of betrayal, but for some reason, the king wanted to question this man himself.

The king eventually asked, "What is your name?"

The young soldier nervously replied, "Your Majesty, my name too is Alexander".

At this, the King was outraged. This traitor shared the name of the great king. Alexander the Great apparently then looked the soldier in the eye and said some chilling words, "Young man, change your life! Or change your name!" The soldier's life was spared, but I'd bet he took the advice.

Jesus was *slightly* more compassionate than Alexander the Great appears to have been, but he is no less a king. In fact, Jesus is the "Lord and God" of the universe. You can't get any more kingly than that! To be a 'Christian'—to respond to Jesus' resurrection—is to bear the name of this great King, Jesus Christ. That demands a change of life in keeping with the name; a life of submission and loyalty to Jesus. In fact, if I claimed to be a 'Christian' and yet had no real loyalty to Christ, I could do with a dose of Alexander's advice to his disloyal soldier–"Change your life! Or change your name!".

The idea of 'submitting' to Jesus or 'being loyal' to Jesus may sound strange to some of us. It simply means following his leadership. Anyone who's ever played competition sport knows how vital it is to follow the coach's leadership. Most of the time, the coach knows best. They are usually highly skilled players themselves. They've often been in the game longer than the players. And they've nearly always got a better view of the match in progress. The higher the level of sport you play, the more true this will be. Whatever the coach says goes! This is not because she, or he, is a grumpy old tyrant. It's because they want the best result for the team, and they know how to get it. So then, if you can imagine Jesus as the ultimate 'high level' coach, and yourself as a player on his team, you are probably getting close to what it means to submit to Jesus.

This, of course, will mean getting to know the instructions Jesus has given his players. Unfortunately, this book can't deal with that massive topic. But if you are interested in knowing more about what Jesus expects of your life, the best thing you could do is read the biographies of Jesus' life for yourself. There you will find his own words about what it means to be loyal to him. The important thing to remember at this point, however, is that responding to Jesus' resurrection in the way he expects us to begins with a decision. Like Thomas, we need to decide that Jesus is our leader–"My Lord and my God!"

Jesus' resurrection does more than simply show us he's the Boss and that we need to treat him as such. It also means that you and I can have real contact with him today. That's what I want to talk about in these last couple of pages.

ALIVE AND KICKING

One of my best mates suggested that the title of this book may leave readers with the impression that Jesus' life was a thing of the past—just another great life that we should remember and take inspiration from. I think he's probably right. Let me assure you, however, that Jesus was not simply a superstar from the past, like Shakespeare, Marilyn Monroe, Elvis or Kurt Cobain. He was not even simply a spiritual hero from the past, like Muhammad, Confucius or Buddha. All of these people are dead and buried. Their lives may have been full of talent, insight and excitement, but it has all gone to the grave with them. Sure, Shakespeare left us some plays; Marilyn some nice photos; Elvis and Kurt some great music; Muhammad, Confucius and Buddha, some profound sayings. But that's about it! With Jesus it's different.

The fact that Jesus was raised from the dead guarantees his ongoing relevance to our lives. Yes, Jesus is a hero of the past, but his resurrection means he is a hero of the present as well. You see, when he was raised from the dead it wasn't to simply live a normal human life, then die again. The biographies make clear that Jesus' resurrection was permanent. It was for keeps.

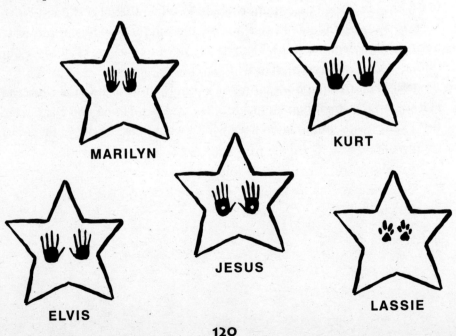

MARILYN

KURT

ELVIS

JESUS

LASSIE

What I am getting at is this: The Jesus written about in the biographies is the same Jesus you and I can relate to now. His talents and achievements are not dead and buried. They are alive and kicking–like him! His powerful teaching, his mastery over evil, his control of the environment, his right to hand out God's forgiveness–these are not just lovely stories written in four ancient books. They are realities right now. The biographies of Jesus tell us not only who Jesus *was,* but also who he *is.* I think it's precisely because Jesus is *now* who he *was then,* that he has remained the true megastar of every century since he walked the earth.

This means you and I, today, can meet Jesus himself. We can literally involve him in our lives, whether at school, uni, work, home or on the sporting field. I guess the question this book ends on is this: do you want to meet this Jesus?

I'm not sure whether you have ever prayed to Jesus, asking him to be real for you now. If not, here is a prayer that may express your desire to know and meet him. Read it through first and if it sounds like the sort of thing you want to say to Jesus, say it! He is alive. He will hear you.

Jesus,
thank you for the great life you lived,
for your teaching, your power and your forgiveness.
Most of all, thank you for dying for me,
for taking my punishment so I could be forgiven.
Please forgive me for my sins.
Give me a clean slate in life.
Thank you also for rising to life.
I realise that you are the true king and leader.
So, please lead my life from this point on.
Teach me how to be loyal to you for as long as I live.
Amen.

CHAPTER

16

A WORD FROM JESUS' FANS

AS I HAVE SAID PREVIOUSLY, Jesus is not simply a thing of the past. Just as he did when he walked the earth, he has continued to make his mark on millions of people throughout the world ever since. You have heard enough of my ravings about the man, so I thought it might be nice to conclude the book with the words of some of my friends. They are also great admirers of Jesus and are living proof that the man who changed world history can also change our personal lives.

DEBRA, 20, UNIVERSITY STUDENT

Jesus is so radically different from the world today. He changes the way I think about everything—my body, my uni exams, money, self-esteem, and how I relate to others. Because of the 'eternal' perspective Jesus gives me, the problems of this life are not so significant. He is often the only person in the world who understands and comforts me, and who loves me even when I'm selfish and angry. His love does not depend on my actions. Jesus has shown me the truth, and that has set me free. I know where I came from, why I am here, and where I am going. I'm stoked!

TIM, 24, NAVAL ARCHITECT

If you asked me who has had the greatest influence in my life, I'd have to say that it was this carpenter who lived 2000 years ago. A carpenter who claimed to be God—a claim that I cannot get past.

I was raised by a Christian family, and did the Sunday school thing. I'm sure some people would say I was indoctrinated by the church and its teachings. But the life Jesus demands from me is hardly the sort of thing you carry out simply because of a childhood teaching. Admittedly, over the years I have at times tried to escape Jesus' claim to be God. But in the end, how do you get past the truth? I can't!

JO, 17 HIGH SCHOOL STUDENT

The love of Jesus is something that I will probably never fully grasp. Through him I have been forgiven and will never have to experience what he did. It's excellent having someone who's always there, is always interested, and who you know is always in control. This gives purpose to my life.

ROBBIE, 28, MARKETING CONSULTANT

In life it is too easy to focus on the wrong things that distract us from the truly beautiful things God created for us all. In my job, I am continually exposed to the demands of the corporate world and this brings imbalance into my life. However, the solution to this, I feel, is to understand how God meant us to live this life. To do this we need to look at Jesus Christ. Through Jesus' life, I can see God's qualities—like his power, greatness and love. Thus, Jesus is my mentor in life. I am always looking forward to applying the ways of Jesus in my personal life and imparting my knowledge and experience to others.

ZOSIA, 14, HIGH SCHOOL STUDENT

The best thing about Jesus is that he sacrificed his life to take away my sins. He took the punishment that should have been mine and gave me something that changed my life forever. Jesus gave me the most important gift ever—the gift of life! By accepting him into my life, I've found new hope and a love that will never end, and a knowledge that he is with me always. Through him, I've become a better person, and by following him I've learnt how to accept my failures and strive to be more like the Jesus I know, who is helping me day by day to change my attitude and my whole life.

BENJAMIN, 29, COLLEGE STUDENT

Even as a young irreligious teenager, the story of Jesus amazed me. His compassion, honesty and love were very striking, and the fact that he carried the cross and died for me, blew me away, and still does every time I think about it.

Although I had previously thought Jesus was totally irrelevant, and that even talking about him was extremely uncool, when I began to look honestly at his life, I was confronted by a completely different bloke to the one I had imagined. And so, at around 14 years of age, whilst in the middle of a 12-month Good Behaviour Bond, I committed my life to Jesus. He has become my saviour and ultimate mate.

FIONA, 34, PROFESSIONAL MUM AND POST-GRADUATE STUDENT

I know how much I love my own children and how much I would do for them. The love and cost of Jesus' sacrifice is beyond my imagination. I am incredibly humbled every time I struggle to forgive someone else and then remember how much Jesus has forgiven me. So I try to live my life for him, to be like him. That might sound restrictive and dull but in actual fact, it makes my life happier in every way because in all situations I can rely on Jesus' wisdom and the hope of his promises.

CYRUS, 16, HIGH SCHOOL STUDENT

For me, the most impressive thing about Jesus' life is his death. He still went through with it even though he knew he was dying for people who would sometimes ignore him, despise him, and even fail to acknowledge his existence.

Jesus means a lot to me in every day life. Firstly, he puts everything in perspective. Because I know where I am going when I die, I am able to put the day to day problems in perspective, and see how small they really are. Jesus also plays a major role in my thinking. He gives me a character guide as to what sort of person I should strive to be.

JACQUES, 27, LANDSCAPE GARDENER

'Freedom' seems to be an icon of the 90s. It's a product that can take us in 'hook, line and sinker'. Often, though, the things we are made to think will give us freedom, turn out to be just empty promises. For me, when I started to follow Jesus, all the things that I previously hung on to for 'freedom'—drugs and other stuff—came to mean nothing. The thrill of those things passed as soon as it came anyway. What I found in Jesus was real freedom, and a great reason to live. When I think of Jesus, I think of just how much he gave—everything! To know that he accepts and loves us completely is what gives us true freedom.

MELISSA, 21, GRAPHIC DESIGNER

Imagine a man who would give up his life for the sin of the world because of his great love for us. Jesus was this man! His incredible sacrifice blew me away, and changed my life. I no longer live my life to please the world, but to serve and please God. And I long to be more like Jesus who is my Lord, my saviour, and my friend.

TONY, 19, UNIVERSITY STUDENT

What impresses me most about Jesus is his ability and willingness to help people in need. He went from town to town doing good and helping people. He brought happiness, joy and healing wherever he went. He loved the unloved, accepted the rejected, and was a friend to those who had no friends.

I believe this Jesus is the same today as he was 2000 years ago. He's in exactly the same business too! That same 'extravagant' love has powerfully touched and changed the lives of myself, my friends, and countless millions of others around the world.

Throughout this book, I have quoted Jesus' words as they are recorded in the Bible. Here's a list of where the quotes come from, in case you want to look them up for yourself.

If you've never read the Bible before, it's broken up into chapters and verses, e.g. Luke 2:15-18 means the book called 'Luke', chapter 2, verses 15-18.

PAGE 24
The account of Jesus' birth is in Luke 2:5-7
The story of the shepherds is in Luke 2:8-20

PAGE 29-30
The Magi appear in Matthew 2

PAGE 36
Jesus' famous words about turning the other cheek are in Matthew 5:39

John the Baptist talks about Jesus in Mark 1:7

PAGE 37
The quote is from Mark 1:22

PAGE 38
The account of the evil spirit is in Mark 1:23-28

PAGES 39-40
Jesus calmed the storm in Mark 4:35-41

PAGES 43-46
The record of Lazarus resurrection is in John 11:17-44

PAGES 51-52 AND 54-55
The story of the healing of the paralysed man is in Mark 2:1-12

PAGES 59-62
The encounter between Simon the Pharisee, the 'sinful woman' and Jesus is in Luke 7:36-50

PAGES 66-67
The Apostles answer Jesus' question "Who do you think I am?" in Mark 8:27-32

PAGES 76-77
The quotes here are from John 14:8-10

PAGES 80-84
The story of Jesus in the Garden of Gethsemane starts at Matthew 26:36

PAGES 87, 89
Jesus' trial is recorded in Mark 15:1-20

PAGES 95-98
Jesus' conversation with the two crucified criminals is in Luke 23:39-43

PAGE 99
Jesus' final words are in Luke 23:44-49

PAGE 117
The record of Jesus' appearance to his Apostles after coming back to life is in John 20:19-28